BLESSED BE
JAZZ

Albums with Fr. Coco's music

A Closer Walk With Three
(With The Ronnie Kole Trio)

Live From St. Louis
An Evening Of Jesuit Jazz

BLESSED BE
JAZZ

The Story of My Life as a Clarinet-Playing Jesuit
Priest in The French Quarter of New Orleans

REV. FRANK COCO, SJ

Acadian House
PUBLISHING
LAFAYETTE, LOUISIANA

ON THE COVER: *Rev. Frank Coco, SJ, (1920-2006) spent the majority of his adult life as a retreat director and high school teacher in south Louisiana, particularly at Jesuit High School in New Orleans, Our Lady of the Oaks Retreat House in Grand Coteau and Manresa Retreat House in Convent. His vocation was that of a Jesuit priest; his avocation was that of a jazz clarinetist. He performed extensively in New Orleans night clubs and other venues, sitting in with some of the best-known jazz musicians of his day.*

Library of Congress Cataloging-in-Publication Data

Coco, Frank, 1920-2006.
  Blessed Be Jazz: The Story of My Life as a Clarinet-Playing Jesuit Priest in The French Quarter of New Orleans / Frank Coco.
      p. cm.
  Includes index.
  ISBN-13: 978-0-925417-89-3 (hardcover)
  ISBN-10: 0-925417-89-0 (hardcover)
  1. Coco, Frank, 1920-2006. 2. Jazz musicians--Louisiana--Biography.
3. Jesuits--Louisiana--Biography. I. Title.

  ML419.C615A3 2009
  781.65092--dc22
  [B]

                    2008049943

♦ Published by Acadian House Publishing, Lafayette, Louisiana
  (Edited by Trent Angers; co-edited by William Kalec;
  produced by Jon Russo)

♦ Cover design by Kevin Pontiff, Lafayette, Louisiana

♦ Printed by Walsworth Printing, Marceline, Missouri

A M D G

Ad majorem Dei gloriam
For the greater glory of God

Let Me Tell You About My Grandchild

T he writing of this book may be rightly considered a presumptuous undertaking. In fact, I toyed with the idea of titling the foreword "Is This Book Necessary?" with a possible subtitle of "Can it serve any earthly purpose?"

Is it possibly an exercise in arrogance? Frank Coco writing a book about Frank Coco? Frank *Who?*

I have been a Jesuit priest of the New Orleans Province for more than thirty-six years, hardly a newsworthy achievement. There is not much merit in mere longevity. About half of those years I spent teaching high school boys at Jesuit High of New Orleans. Nothing momentous about that. During the other half, roughly, I have been engaged in giving retreats in southeast and southwest Louisiana – a fact that hardly cries out to be recorded for posterity.

This book is not about my calling to the priesthood and the two ministries that have been my chief occupation during those years. No, it is not about my vocation; it is about my avocation.

At the age of eleven I fell in love with the clarinet in Helena, Arkansas, a town on the Mississippi, about fifty miles down-river from Memphis, Tennessee. At Sacred Heart Academy in Helena, Sr. Agnes Cecilia, SCN, an admirable music teacher, tutored me carefully and lovingly. I drove my parents and eight brothers and sisters to distraction by practicing at close quarters four or five hours a day. My transition to the tenor sax was easy for me, but even more exasperating for them.

In 1933, at age thirteen, I landed a job (thanks to my oldest brother, Sam, a trumpet player) playing sax and clarinet in a swing band, The Lou Bell Orchestra. Lou was an osteopath, a tall gangling man from Oklahoma, who fronted the band with a violin – but without the grace of Guy Lombardo – and was later persuaded to retire to the rear on bass fiddle. I was the only non-adult in the band.

The Lou Bell Orchestra broke up a few years later, and I wound up in the only other dance band in town, The Seaporters, so named because of Helena's identification as "Arkansas' only seaport."

My "professional career" ended abruptly at age seventeen when I left home to join the Jesuits, arriving at the novitiate in Grand Coteau, Louisiana, in July of 1938. Among my possessions was my beloved Albert System clarinet, purchased by my brother Sam, after some haggling worthy of a Persian market, in a pawnshop on Beale Street in Memphis. I had had to sell my tenor sax to help finance my trip to the Jesuit novitiate. My clarinet was my link to the past and the wondrous world of popular music out there "in the world."

In those days the discipline of the Jesuit Order precluded any thought of my ever playing in a public setting again, but I had every intention of continuing to play the clarinet as long as I had breath and reeds. In the liner notes on the back of the only album I have ever recorded, I referred to "…the frustration of many years of performing before imaginary audiences in Fantasy Hall."

But in the '60s, along came Pope John XXIII, who "opened windows to let fresh air into the Church," and I crawled through one of those windows, out into the jazz public.

The decision of that saintly man to "open windows" released me into the world of the kind of music I had never ceased to love. It happened during my teaching years at Jesuit High in New Orleans.

In the spring of 1965 I met the musician I had come to revere when he was performing with Lawrence Welk on national television – the incomparable clarinetist, Pete Fountain. We met in the back room of his Bourbon Street nightclub. My admiration for Pete was so great that on Mardi Gras day, I ran a couple of blocks to catch up with his Half-Fast Walking Club – just to get a glimpse of him with his cavorting walkers.

By 1966 we had become friends and I had become chaplain

of the Half-Fast Walking Club, a position I have been privileged to hold ever since.

Once I was through the window and out into the jazz public I began to meet the outstanding jazz musicians with whom New Orleans is so blessed. They began to invite me to sit in with their bands. As I met more and more jazz musicians, more and more open invitations to sit in and play a few tunes came my way. Through a little enterprising on my part, this happened in other cities I came to live in and visit. And I am still at it.

Now in my mid-sixties, I find myself more and more often looking back over those years. I regret not having kept a journal of the events and impressions of years gone by. That may well have made the onus of writing this book lighter, but write it I must. There are so many memories weltering in the depths of my mind that I feel have to be fished up, organized and displayed – for my own satisfaction, if not for anyone else's.

So I will do it.

Of course, the dark temptation of self-doubt besets me as I begin. All this is of great interest to *me*. *I* cherish all the memories, but who else is interested? Who else cares? The temptation of self-doubt afflicts the best. Thomas Wolfe wrote touchingly of it.

Some of my brother Jesuits and friends and relatives, however, have assured me that this project has merit. My superiors have allotted sabbatical time and given encouragement to indicate that they believe in it.

Yet, I still have that deep-seated suspicion that I am like a grandfather trying to corner listeners to hear about the fascinating exploits and virtues of his grandchild.

So be it. Let me get on with it. Let me tell you about my grandchild.

– Rev. Frank Coco, SJ

Acknowledgements

This book came together, as most books do, with the help of many people, some of whom we acknowledge here.

Thanks to those who were more than willing to share their Fr. Coco stories, photos and memories. They include: Dr. George Bourgeois and his daughter Rachal, Dr. Donald Faust, Pete Fountain, Bob Guchereau, Dr. Steve and Joan Herbert, Kathlyn Hurst, Ronnie Kole, Joe Lamendola, Dr. Wilmot and Janette Ploger and Dr. Jay Michael Rooney. Also, our gratitude to John Shoup, Amy Patselikos and Susan R. Countess, who provided key photos to us in the eleventh hour.

As she has with many of our book projects, Darlene Smith thoroughly reviewed the text and corrected errors in grammar, punctuation and the like. Fr. Raymond Fitzgerald, SJ, checked it for factual error.

The staff of Acadian House Publishing worked long hours on the project. Graphic artist Jon Russo produced the book. Matt Abshire proofed all 26 chapters. Kim Krabill had the daunting task of retyping most of Fr. Coco's manuscript to create the electronic file we needed.

Finally, we'd like to thank Fr. Coco's brother, Bro. Anthony Coco, SJ, who helped with various aspects of the book, providing photos and old newspaper clippings and putting us in touch with close friends of Fr. Coco.

– The Editors

Table of Contents

BLESSED BE
JAZZ

Note on the time frame of this book

The majority of the chapters of this book were written in 1987 and 1988, while Fr. Coco was on sabbatical leave. He wrote while hunkered down at the Weston Jesuit School of Theology in Cambridge, Mass., free from his normal responsibilities.

The last three or four chapters were written in 1992 and 1993 and possibly later, while he was stationed at Our Lady of the Oaks Retreat House in Grand Coteau, La.

CHAPTER 1

Blessed Be Jazz!

*B*ETH RENGEL, YOUNG, ATTRACTIVE AND competent, had come from Baton Rouge to Manresa House of Retreats in Convent, Louisiana – which is on the River Road about halfway between Baton Rouge and New Orleans – to do a story for a Baton Rouge TV station.

Manresa serves mainly three dioceses in south Louisiana, but attracts men from many other areas who want to enter its world of peace, quiet and beauty. Catholics, Protestants, Jews – any men of goodwill, with any degree of faith in God – are welcome to spend the three days of silence, reflection and prayer; to attend talks centered largely on the teachings and way of life of Jesus Christ as applied to modern life; to seek advice and counseling from the four Jesuit priests on duty during the retreat. Manresa draws more than five thousand men a year.

The stately, white-columned, antebellum main building is a photographer's delight. The other buildings and the lovely grounds are eminently photogenic. It was my privilege to live with and minister to the people of God in this setting for seven years.

I was on the scene when Beth and her crew came to tape the Manresa story and stumbled on another story – mine. She, her crew and the Jesuit staff were on a lunch break in our little dining room. It was obvious that she was not Catholic and had had little experience associating with Roman Catholic priests and was interested in exploring that small *terra incognita*.

"What do you do when you're not engaged in retreat work? I mean what do you do for recreation? Do you have any pastimes, hobbies?"

Fr. Duval Hilbert, director of Manresa, volunteered an answer:

"Fr. Cronin and Fr. Kissinger are golfers. And you're sitting next to a man who gets his kicks playing jazz clarinet in the French Quarter. He's a personal friend of Pete Fountain, chaplain of Pete's Half-Fast Walking Club, walks with them every Mardi Gras…"

She was amazed, and a barrage of questions followed.

"Where do you play? With whom? When?"

The question, however, that stopped me was, "How do you reconcile this with being a priest?"

Frankly, I had never given that much thought, but I could see the source of her problem – pseudo-problem, really. The stereotype of the priest, or any "man of the cloth" for that matter, simply seemed irreconcilable with the image of a jazz clarinetist on a French Quarter bandstand in black suit and Roman collar (which I always wear for a public appearance, except when I am costumed with the Walking Club on Mardi Gras Day).

I do not recall exactly how I answered her question, or if I did answer it to her satisfaction. I know I reminded her that God is everywhere – even on Bourbon Street. That I had no intention of conforming to anyone's narrow image of the priesthood. That I saw no difficulty in being a good priest and being myself. That the musicians I sat in with, the waiters and waitresses, bartenders and customers were generally pleased with my presence and respected me as priest and musician. And that my Jesuit superiors fully endorsed my activity.

The upshot was, "I think I have another story here." Indeed she did, and she returned a few months later to do it. An interview was videotaped at Manresa. Shots of me in action were taken at the altar and at the lectern during a retreat in progress. More action shots of "the jazz priest" with the Ronnie Kole Trio. I recall now that my aged clarinet was in the repair shop, and I disappointed her by playing the tenor sax that evening.

The TV segment was smartly and professionally done. It was well received. For me, however, the best thing that came out of it was the title she gave it – a stroke of genius! – "Blessed Be Jazz."

I like it. I believe it. I have used it in greetings and with autographs. I have appropriated it as the title of this book.

And to Beth Rengel, the TV reporter, wherever you are, I say God bless you and thank you, my dear.

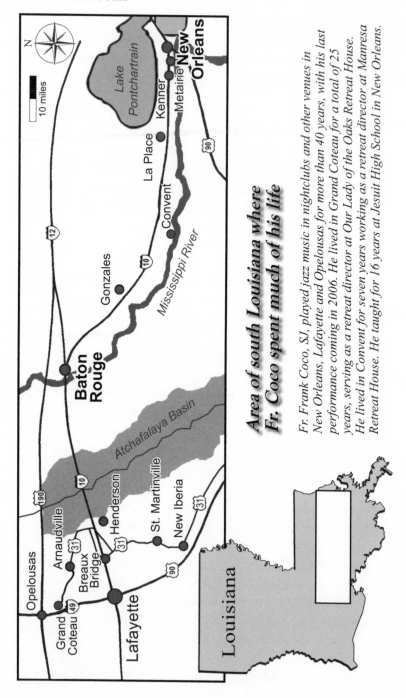

*Area of south Louisiana where
Fr. Coco spent much of his life*

Fr. Frank Coco, SJ, played jazz music in nightclubs and other venues in New Orleans, Lafayette and Opelousas for more than 40 years, with his last performance coming in 2006. He lived in Grand Coteau for a total of 25 years, serving as a retreat director at Our Lady of the Oaks Retreat House. He lived in Convent for seven years working as a retreat director at Manresa Retreat House. He taught for 16 years at Jesuit High School in New Orleans.

CHAPTER 2

Why is Pete Fountain behind me?

*I*AM IN THE NEW ORLEANS HILTON. I AM ON the third floor. I am in Pete Fountain's club. Pete catches the bartender's eye and nods.

As Pete's band continues to play, I follow the bartender, ever-faithful Paul Famiglia, clarinet in case under my arm. Paul opens the side door, and I am backstage nervously assembling my clarinet. I moisten my reed and blow a few notes in the low register, playing what I am hearing from the bandstand. Just a few phrases, and softly. It's okay. The horn's playing just fine. No nightmarish malfunction is going to happen.

I hear the concluding strains of the number. I hear Pete's voice: "…my good buddy, Fr. Coco…" My cue. I come through the back curtains, smile and nod right and left to the musicians, say hello to Pete as I pass him and take my position front and center at the mic.

The pianist, the talented Earl Vuiovich, is improvising an intro, waiting for me to jump in. I hit the first notes of "Summertime." The band comes in behind me, a solid wall of support and inspiration.

And Pete, playing quietly along, is *behind* me! Pete Fountain, behind *me*!

This is not a dream. This is really happening. It has happened many times. Here it is happening again.

Pete Fountain stands behind me, Frank Coco, a son of Sicilian immigrants who, with his eight brothers and sisters, grew up in Helena, Arkansas, in the back of a corner grocery store. Who discovered the clarinet at the age of eleven. Who, at a tender age, heard New Orleans jazz on the excursion boats out of New Orleans, the end of an era. They all stopped at Helena. The calliope playing during the day sent the message all over town: "Come dance on the river tonight!" A little budding clarinetist, too young to be interested in dancing, standing by the band all night, not aware of what he was listening to but lost in the wonder of the glorious sound. He missed Satchmo by a few years, but heard Fate Marable, not knowing yet who either was.

Tonight I am in New Orleans, playing New Orleans-style, with one of the world's greatest exponents of the art standing behind me. *Things that cannot be but are.*

All is going very well. The band is solid behind me. Pete is doodling prettily back there, and I am riding on their shoulders. I am making my way through three choruses of "Summertime." People are listening. I think, *They probably didn't expect much...* I am trying to put an original stamp on each chorus, trying to avoid too many clichés on the way.

Now I have finished my three choruses and I step back to where Pete is. He smiles and says a few encouraging words as master guitarist Lloyd Ellis takes over the melody and has his shot at a couple of choruses.

There are two glasses of wine on the piano. For some reason, there always are. Pete hands me one and lifts the other and we nod in a mutual toast. The crowd responds gleefully.

As the final soloist comes to the end of his last chorus, Pete nods towards the front mic, which means "Your turn again." I do a couple of additional choruses and then we ride it out with a strong *fortissimo* chorus. At the end I am groping my way through a short *cadenza*, always different but, to me, never quite what I want it to say. But I'm happy to emerge from the dead silence without a squeak or a false note. A big smashing final chord from the whole band and it's over. We then Dixieland our way through an upbeat version of "Margie."

I leave the bandstand and I am backstage again as the band breaks out into a rousing version of "The Saints," featuring the remarkable drummer Charlie Lodice. I am coming back down to earth as I disassemble my clarinet and put it back in the case, but I am still thinking, *Is this really real?*

I float back to my seat and listen and think, *I was up there!*

CHAPTER 3

I Meet 'The Man'

*I*DISCOVERED PETE FOUNTAIN IN THE LATE 1950s on television, on the very popular *Lawrence Welk Show*. I said to myself, *Where has this man been all my life?*

I could not believe my ears. He was from New Orleans, already playing brilliantly in his teens as a student at Warren Easton High School. His school was just a dozen or so blocks from Jesuit High, where and when (the mid-'40s) I was teaching as a young Jesuit. So how is it I had never heard of him?

I never missed a *Lawrence Welk Show*, always listening impatiently for Pete to come on, knowing that he would be near the end of the program. After he departed the show to return to New Orleans, I was left with a consuming desire to hear him live and meet him some day. But I lost track of him.

I subsequently learned that Pete, on his return, had gone to work for club owner Dan Levy at Pier 600 in the

French Quarter. Pete enjoyed instant success. The tourists, who knew him, as millions did, from *The Lawrence Welk Show*, flocked to hear him play. I doubt that Pete had any idea how well-known he had become nationally. Pete Fountain is a very unassuming man.

Pete had the greatest respect for Dan Levy and was very satisfied with all the working conditions – with one notable exception. Pete insisted on two days off per week. Dan said he could not grant this. Pete's position reflected one of the traits I admire in him: He is a family man.

Dan and Pete eventually parted company. Within a year, in 1961, Pete had his own club in the Quarter, Pete Fountain's French Quarter Inn, on the corner of Bourbon Street and St. Ann. It was there that I re-discovered him, in the spring of 1965, heard him play live for the first time in my life, and met him.

I had known that Pete was performing at his French Quarter Inn, but was a bit leery in those days about showing my face (and Roman collar) on Bourbon Street late at night. (I have since recovered fully from that feeling.) Hearing Pete Fountain play in his club, therefore, remained a wistful dream – until one happy evening when I was having dinner at the home of friends.

There was a set of drums in the living room. Both "Pudgy" and his son loved to play them. I was jamming on clarinet with "Pudge" that evening after dinner. I spoke of my admiration for Pete Fountain. "Pudge" was surprised that I had never heard Pete live.

"My wife and I will take you to dinner some evening, and after dinner we'll take in Pete Fountain's show."

"I don't know. How do you think a Roman collar would look in a French Quarter nightclub? I don't know," I said.

"No problem. You're in New Orleans, man."

I was reassured. We went.

It was (God forgive me!) on Ash Wednesday in 1965. No sooner had we been seated than a friend, the father of a young man studying for the Jesuit priesthood, noticed me and came to our table, his forehead still smudged with the ritual ashes of the Church. (Where else but in New Orleans!) I immediately felt at home.

"Well, Fr. Coco! What in the world are you doing here?"

The question was, of course, rhetorical.

"I've come to hear Pete Fountain live for the first time in my life. I'm really excited."

"Would you like to meet him after the show?"

"I'd love to."

"I've known Pete since he was a child. I'll introduce him to you after the show."

My cup was was not just running over, it was flooding the place!

I remember the show starting with a warmup number featuring the great vibes man, Godfrey Hirsch. Then Pete joined the band, and suddenly I was no longer on planet Earth. The man and the horn were one reality of glorious sound, and I was swept up and away with it. For an hour and a half I lived in Never-Never Land.

The back room at the club was on the second floor. The passage of many, many years since I climbed that flight of stairs has not erased the sense of awe I experienced that night.

Pete and I shook hands and sat down to talk. Predictably, the discussion was about our mutual interest in jazz music and clarinets. We began talking about clarinet reeds. Reeds. The agony and ecstasy of clarinetists. Often agony as you test and discard poor ones, or when a good one splits on you or just plays out. It is like the death of a friend and reliable companion. A great instrument, great talent and great training all hang on the thread of a little piece of cane that rests on the facing of the mouthpiece. (Now, mouthpieces are another story.) Buying a box of clarinet reeds is like going on a fishing or hunting trip. In fact, "hunting" for a good reed is jazz jargon.

Our first conversation began something like this:

"I'm a clarinetist, Pete, and I want to ask you one question: How do you get good reeds?"

"I have the same problem finding good reeds as anybody else does. I think those Frenchmen who cut those reeds must be drinking too much wine on the job. When I was a kid you could get good reeds, but I didn't have any money to buy 'em. Now everybody wants to give me reeds, their brand, and it's tough to find good ones. I've been using Bonades. What strength reed do you use?"

"Two and a half."

"Here, you may find a few good ones in this box."

He tossed me a box of Bonades, unopened, still sealed.

The gesture was so characteristic of the Pete Fountain I came to know, a man who delights in giving. A friend of Pete, a musician, once told me he expressed admiration for a set of cuff links Pete was wearing, and Pete promptly took them off and handed them over.

The clarinet I play today is a gift from Pete Fountain. One evening he suggested (tongue-in-cheek) that I donate my old Albert system clarinet – which my brother purchased for me in a pawnshop – to the Cabildo (a New Orleans museum).

"I can find you a better Albert than that one."

The Albert system, once described (with some exaggeration) as "a Model-T Ford," is no longer manufactured. One learns today on the improved Boehm system.

He did come up with a good Albert, a Conn, and presented it to me at his nightclub. Long before that, on learning that I did not own a tenor saxophone, he gave me one – but that is a story in itself, which I will tell later.

The second time I spoke to Pete was during the intermission of a benefit for which he was playing. It was, I think, for Mt. Carmel High, his daughter's alma mater.

I boldly knocked on the dressing room door.

"Come in. Oh, come on in, Father. How's the reed situation?"

"Okay."

"How about a drink?"

I was at the beginning of a long and cherished friendship.

CHAPTER 4

Pete Fountain's Half-Fast Walking Club

A Toast

Here's to the braves and the great Chief of Jazz!
They're not true-bred Indians, not even half-cast;
They're not really loaded, no more than half-gassed;
Their ambition's not mighty, but only half-vast;
Their pace is not speedy, but only half-fast;
But as whole-hearted buddies they can't be surpassed!

I wrote these verses the year I accepted the invitation to join Pete Fountain's Walking Club as their first chaplain. It was an attempt to express how I felt (and still feel) about these men whom I love, with whom I have been associated for more than twenty-four years, with whom I have walked in the Mardi Gras parade for twenty-four successive years.

Our costumes vary from year to year. In my first year (1966) we walked as American Indians; hence the reference to "Chief" and "braves." Incidentally, although I generally wear clerical garb in public settings, I lay it aside on Mardi Gras Day and don the costume of the day to walk with my Half-Fast buddies.

Pete Fountain's Walking Club is not a musical organization. Most of the members are not musicians. It is a men's social club whose primary function of the year is walking in the Mardi Gras Day parade.

We are not, as we are often mistakenly dubbed, a *marching* club. Far from it. The word connotes discipline and precision, neither of which interests us. We *walk*.

We walk not only on Mardi Gras Day but at other times, for other occasions. We have walked in the St. Patrick's Day parade, for instance, and we have been part of a combined public tribute to both St. Patrick and St. Joseph, walking with Irish-American and Italian-American celebrants on a Sunday in March, the feast days of these two saints falling, respectively, on March 17 and March 19. We also walk occasionally in grand ballrooms of hotels to entertain delighted conventioneers. And once, I recall, at a Super Bowl.

There are, of course, the usual activities typical of any social club, such as the annual Christmas dance, picnics, crawfish boils and dinners. Once in a while there is a special function, as when the members convened to eat, drink and view the premiere showing on public television of an hour-length documentary on the musical life of our Chief, or, to give him his proper title, our Grand Marshal.

New Orleanians are a parade-happy people. Pete Fountain's Walking Club came out of that deep-seated tradition. Its official birth-year is 1961. But well before that year Pete and his wife-to-be and a number of his friends and their dates, all in costumes, walked the parade route (or part of it) without invitation, permit or organization.

It became an exclusively male organization because, as Pete once observed (in jest?), the women were embarrassing the men by out-walking them. Be it said, to her everlasting credit, that Beverly, Pete's lovely wife, subtly indicated her disdain for the men and their organization by giving the Walking Club its present name.

We celebrated our silver anniversary in 1986 by walking in the Mardi Gras parade on a frigid February day in "silver" (actually pale gray) tuxedos, complete with top hats and tails, a dignified variation from the pirates, sombreroed Mexicans, Canadian Mounties, Minute Men and Vikings of previous years.

We walk next as clowns.

"So what's new?" This from one of our members at the meeting when the choice of costumes was announced.

The experience of walking with the Walking Club on Mardi Gras Day defies description. The mirth and camaraderie of the members, the thousands of people who line the parade route eager to see, listen and catch the "doubloons" we throw; the music of the jazz musicians clustered around Pete and his black-and-gold clarinet in the vanguard; Art Ryder's jazz band that brings up the rear; the banner boys (privileged youngsters, usually sons or nephews of the members); our captain, "Wimpy" Courrege, bustling about like an NBA referee, whistle at the ready – all of it one glorious mélange of sound and color. And the multitudes love it.

We rendezvous early in the morning on the patio of Commander's Palace, one of New Orleans' finest restaurants, located in the Garden District, a few miles from the French Quarter. There is a sense of eagerness and expectancy in the air as we mill around. I am with a group of children, and am one of them, on Christmas Eve. That comes closest to describing the feeling I experience each year.

Wimpy is now blowing his importunate whistle. The word passes along.

"We're moving out, we're moving out. Let's go."

We file out onto Washington Avenue and fall in behind

Pete and the banner boys. Now Wimpy's persistent whistle is calling for silence. The word passes all around: "Quiet! Quiet!" I will start the walk with a prayer.

The men doff their headgear and bow their heads. I say one of the versions of an old Irish prayer:

"May the Lord walk with us this day. May He be in front of us to guide us; behind us to guard us; above us to bless us; within us to sustain us...."

With a couple of blasts of Wimpy's whistle and the thunderous beat of the snare and bass drums, we're off!

Soon one of the bands jumps into a lively jazz number and the people lining the avenue respond. Although it is early, not yet 8 a.m., and we are five or six blocks from St. Charles Avenue (the parade route), the number of people is already considerable. Many move along with us, block after block, and all are clapping their hands in time with the music, some even dancing along the way, heads bobbing, arms swinging and torsos weaving, the primitive, joyous strut of New Orleans "second-liners."

A surge of gladness comes over me in the realization that we are spreading joy, bringing a little sunshine into the hearts and to the faces of thousands upon thousands for five or six solid hours. Mardi Gras has been called the "Greatest Free Show On Earth." There are abuses and one sees them along the way, but why bow to the minority? The vast majority of the people – and they add up to millions – that I have seen in my twenty-four walks are good, decent people out to have a good time, and I, priest of God though I be, am happy to be able to bring a bit of cheer into their lives.

CHAPTER 5

My French Quarter Debut

*D*URING THE MANY YEARS THAT I HAVE BEEN on the New Orleans jazz scene, I have met and played with a multitude of musicians. Many are still alive, a few have retired, some have died. But all of them, and all the joyful moments I have had with them, be they performances or conversations, are filed in the archives of my mind.

Psychologists tell us that every human experience is permanently recorded in the human mind. Bringing these experiences up into the light of consciousness is quite another matter.

It is consoling to know that all those musicians and all those moments of joy are on permanent record. I wish I could introduce you to all the musicians in my past and share with you the moments of joy I had with them. I fear, however, that I will have to settle for much less than that. I apologize in advance to the musicians I know I will inevitably overlook.

I will never forget my first appearance on a French

33

Quarter bandstand. It was at The Famous Door, on the corner of Bourbon and Conti, in the late 1960s. Under the ownership and management of the legendary Hyp Guinle, the place featured great Dixieland jazz bands that were drawing large and enthusiastic crowds in those days. Dixieland jazz was enjoying a re-emergence after years of being eclipsed by the big bands of the swing era.

The Famous Door featured continuous music. Two bands alternated, closing and opening each set with a chorus or two of "Way Down Yonder in New Orleans." The members of the band going off left singly, replaced one by one by the members of the band coming on, with "Way Down Yonder..." continuing to be played in the displacement process. The only breaks in the action all night were the brief pauses between tunes. Unfortunately, today's economy will not permit such a luxury.

The tradition of continuous jazz was still very much alive when I first walked into The Famous Door, though, sadly, Hyp Guinle was not. I deeply regret that I never met him. Hyp died in 1965. His gracious wife – "Aunt G," she was called – was managing the club when I first came.

It was at the invitation of her nephew, Nick Campo, who was a student in my senior honors class at Jesuit High School. Today he is Dr. Nick Campo, a physician practicing internal medicine in the New Orleans area. I will be forever grateful to him for initiating what has proven to be happy therapy through the years.

I came at his invitation to listen to two excellent Dixieland bands, one under the leadership of trombonist Santo Pecora, one of the pioneers of Dixieland jazz. The renowned bandleader Jan Garber, whom I once met at The Famous Door, was an admirer of Santo Pecora's playing. He had come to hear Santo, too.

I did not dream that I would be on the bandstand with giants that night, invited to sit in. (New Orleans jazz musicians rarely literally sit, if they are horn players.)

The drummer in one of the bands was Darryl Prechter, a spectacular young player whom I had met a few weeks earlier. We had walked and played together on Mardi Gras Day with Pete Fountain's famed Half-Fast Walking Club. Darryl was, for a while, a member of Pete's band.

A smile and a wave of the hand from Darryl acknowledged my presence. What I did not realize was that he had informed the leader of one of the bands that "Father can play," and he suggested that I be invited to sit in. Unfortunately, I had not brought my clarinet with me.

The two clarinets on the bandstand were of the Boehm system. And while I had learned on the Boehm, it was the Albert clarinet I had been playing most of my adult life.

Fortunately, I was also experienced in playing the tenor sax, and that's what I was asked to play that night – which I did gladly.

The musicians were pleased. The crowd's response – after, I am sure, some initial shock at seeing a black-suited, Roman-collared sax player on the bandstand – was warm. And I was on a cloud of joy.

This was the first of many invitations and many happy moments at The Famous Door and other clubs and lounges in New Orleans, where to this day I have an open invitation to sit in. That initial invitation was, in the words of a popular song, "the start of something good."

On the façade of The Famous Door there are rows of names printed in white on a black background, names of musicians who have performed or celebrities who have visited this citadel of traditional jazz. I am surely no celebrity, but my name is on one of those plaques – up there next to that of Archbishop Hannan. I see in this display the kindness of Mrs. Hyp Guinle, "Aunt G," and cherish it as a private memorial of my French Quarter debut.

CHAPTER 6

Heaven's All-Star Band

*T*HERE IS SUCH A NUMBER OF JAZZ MUSICIANS in the hold of my memory that I despair of ever bringing them all up and giving them their due. In spite of that, I am driven to have a go at it.

I will begin by summoning up, one at a time, those whom I can recall who are no longer on planet Earth.

Front and center, trombonist **Santo Pecora**, you shared your bandstand with me, an amateur player, and made me feel at home up there. Tall, handsome and admired by Jan Garber and even Tommy Dorsey, your rich tones were heard on the first Dixieland jazz recording ever. I can still hear that jazzy version of "Liebestraum" flowing from the golden bell of your horn. Rest in peace!

Front and center, **Frankie Assunto**, showman, trumpet man, jazz singer. The last leader of the original Dukes of Dixieland, with your father, the beloved "Papa Jac," and your gifted brother Freddie and his wife Betty "The Duchess," (who can still belt out "Bill Bailey" with the best), you were once the toast of Las Vegas and one of the best Dixieland combos ever to come out of New Orleans. Although it has been fifteen years, I have, engraved in my memory, the image of you a month before your death, the last time I saw you. Not working, drink in hand, trumpet under your arm, you walked into the Maison Bourbon. I was shocked at the way you looked. The shades of death were coming down, although I did not guess it. That obituary in *The Times-Picayune* chilled my soul. But there was life in the sound of your horn that evening, Frankie, as we shared the bandstand and jammed with my good friend and accomplished jazz cornetist, Connie Jones. Rest in peace!

Walk on, **Paul Barbarin**, leader of the fabled Onward Brass Band, extraordinary drummer, immortalized in the jazz classic you composed, "Bourbon Street Parade." You died in action, dropping out of that night parade on the eve of Mardi Gras, and did not live to walk with us and your Onward brothers the following morning. But the Half-Fast Walking Club walked and the Onward brothers walked and your spirit walked with us that day. I led a prayer for your soul that morning. Rest in peace "in that number," Paul Barbarin!

Louie, Onward's great clarinetist, **Louie Cottrell**, you did walk with us that day, but not many years later, as you too walked on into eternity. I can still see you, the sweat beading upon your brow under the bill of your black and white band cap. You were tall, portly, a blissful smile on your face, shambling along, the bell of your old Albert clarinet nearly resting on your ample front, the sure notes tumbling out. You logged many tedious parade miles in your day. So rest in peace!

Come out, **Russell Mayne**, born in Opelousas, Louisiana, your life senselessly snuffed out by a bullet in Lafayette, Louisiana, when you came to the aid of your step-daughter. Small, soft-spoken, a giant at the keyboard, who would want to hurt you? You did not have it in you to hurt anyone. All that music – ragtime, traditional jazz, contemporary – all that wizardry vanished that morning. I recall that remarkable jam session at your home that went into the wee hours of the morning with your good friend and mine, superb alto saxophonist Al Belletto. The later it went, the better it became, so that I began to feel like a dwarf between giants and quietly put my clarinet back in the case and sat back to listen and learn. I cherish the memory of the very last night I heard you play. You made one of your infrequent appearances at one of those swinging Wednesday night jam sessions at Toby's in Lafayette. You rocked the rafters. Then, as always, you tried to make me feel that I belonged on the bandstand with you, but I knew better. I meant what I said at that sad double funeral: "I was a scooter trying to run with a freight train." Rest in peace!

Bob Coquille, "a gentleman and a gentle man" I called you when I spoke at your funeral Mass. You were both. You are in my earliest memories of sitting in at The Famous Door, your rock-solid, steady bass behind me, never in the way. The last night we played together you were on the bandstand at The Door when you should have been home in bed with the illness that was soon to take you from us. Faithful and loving family man, steady musician, gentle friend. Rest in peace!

Earl Vuiovich, come take a well-deserved bow. Twenty-seven years at the keyboard with Pete Fountain's band, the "backbone of the organization," as Pete loved to call you. How well we came to realize that after you left this world. I marvelled at the delicate touch of your fresh and impeccable solos. I rode on the security of your accompaniment, as we did "Summertime" and "Margie," as secure as a child on his father's knee. Humble, lovable artist, we miss you. Rest in peace!

Take a bow, dear **Pee Wee Spitelera**, star clarinetist with

Al Hirt's band for – how many years? Close to twenty, I think. I can see you now on the bandstand, short, roly-poly, head moving quickly from side to side as you played. I can see those pudgy fingers flying over the golden keys as you ripped off "Struttin' with Some Barbecue," warming to the task as you moved on, chorus after chorus, chasing those marvelous variations that came rolling out. I can hear you wailing the blues, all heart, all New Orleans. Your rendition of "Creole Love Song," I am told, caught the ear of Duke Ellington.

You weathered a heart attack and a bypass operation and came back to the bandstand before the physicians thought you should. (I know you talked them into it.) Later you fought back after a stroke and returned yet again to play. When Al Hirt formed his Big Band (a short-lived venture) and hit the road, he left a superb Dixieland clarinetist behind. You gigged around here and there "on the street" and then dismayed me when you decided to quit playing. We talked about it. You asked for my prayers. Now my prayers and my love follow you into eternity, gone from us at too young an age.

But my fondest memory of you is not a musical one, though I have stored many of those. It was an act of kindness. I was on Keith Rush's morning talk show. I had come on his show to solicit donations of second-hand musical instruments for a school band in Sri Lanka (then Ceylon), a mission school manned by my fellow Southern Jesuits. You heard the appeal on your car radio, parked and called the station from a pay phone.

"I have a pretty good clarinet at home that you can have. All it needs is a mouthpiece. How can I get it to you?"

"Bring it to the club. I'm coming in to hear you guys tonight," I said. (I might have added "and sit in," for the great Al Hirt would graciously invite me to do so whenever I came in.)

I am thinking that in that Asian country, torn these days

by civil violence and hatred, there is a clarinet somewhere that came from a loving and loveable little man with a big tone and a big heart. Rest in peace, Pee Wee. I miss you.

Jack Delaney, come front and center, as I often saw you do in Pete Fountain's band when you sang "Do You Know What It Means To Miss New Orleans?" You sang it your way, remarkably mimicking the incomparable Louie Armstrong. I had intended to ask you why, after Louie's death, you stopped mimicking his voice. Was it out of reverence for his greatness? Knowing you well, I think it was. I wanted to discuss that with you, but never got around to it.

I was told that even in your freshman year at Jesuit High you were already a good Satchmo sound-alike and the pride of Prof. Michael Cupero's trombone section – until you washed out of school because jazz meant more to you than textbooks. Yet you doggedly pursued and finally achieved – with a boost from Fr. Ed Doyle, SJ, of Loyola of the South, to whom you were ever grateful – your ambition to finish your education and qualify as a grade school teacher. When you made it, you did not know that you had so little time left to pursue your double career.

I recall your final struggle, valiantly playing your trombone, mouthpiece pressed at the left corner of your mouth, because of the location of the cancer that was closing in on you. Then later, no longer able to play, still on Pete's payroll, you worked in the back, at the club's service bar.

Dear humble, shy Jack Delaney, who would wince whenever a musician or employee let slip a profanity in earshot of "the Father." You were more uncomfortable than I.

I was not scheduled and so not prepared to deliver the eulogy at your funeral Mass. But when the priest from your parish church, who celebrated the Mass, confided to me that he did not know you personally and offered me the opportunity, I knew I had to speak. Someone had to say something personal about you. I spoke, but not as well as you deserved. Let these words stand as a second chorus of praise for you. Rest in peace, dear Jack.

Rest in peace all of you! Santo, Frankie, Paul, Louie, Russell, Bob, Earl, Pee Wee and Jack. And for the countless hours of pleasure you gave me through the years and for your kindness, thank you.

What an all-star band we have up there!

CHAPTER 7

The Wonderful Electric Sound Wagon

*I*F YOU HAPPEN TO CATCH THE HALF-FAST Walking Club on Mardi Gras Day, you will see not only walkers but two interesting vehicles. The first, to be discussed in this chapter, is Art Ryder's Wonderful Electric Sound Wagon; the second, described in the next chapter, is what we affectionately refer to as The Mystery Chariot.

Neither vehicle is designed to carry people. Unless they are disabled, all members are expected to walk. We make provision, too, for members too old to walk but who still want to be with the group on Mardi Gras Day.

Pete Fountain's father, the beloved "Pops," reached a point, a few years before he died, of having to ride, much to his dismay. Courageous Leo Bowen, a retired police officer, victimized by a serious stroke, will most likely never walk the route again, but he rides along with us every year. The rest of us walk.

Art Rider's Wonderful Electric Sound Wagon is a miracle of ingenuity that has rolled at the rear of the Walking

Club for years. It is a homemade mobile sound system. Art and his band members call it "The War Wagon."

The wagon had a humble beginning. In its infancy it was a discarded grocery shopping cart. Mounted on it was one battery, powering a single speaker. Two mics served all the members of a six-piece band. This vehicle was pulled along parade routes long before Art Ryder and his band began to walk with Pete's club, but has long since been retired.

The wagon today is an intriguing contraption that is a marvel to behold – and hear.

Credit for the concept goes to Henri Guerineau, formerly a trumpet player in Art's band. With Art and with the aid of Art's friend, Paul Daigle, that concept came to be the reality that rolls so grandly with us on Mardi Gras Day. It has, Art claims, been imitated but never duplicated.

At the bottom of the wagon is a cut-down boat trailer resting on a balloon-tired dolly. Surmounting this understructure is "the tower," which rises to about five or six feet. Atop it is a cluster of four speakers that project, to unlimited volume, the sound of the horns – trumpets, trombones, clarinets.

Two amplifiers at the bottom of the tower carry the sound of the rhythm instruments.

The whole system is powered by four active batteries, with two more in reserve, at the ready.

There are three mics, jutting out on goosenecks, at the rear of the vehicle and one at each side up front.

The whole rig measures roughly four feet in width and in length. By way of an added feature, a siren, retrieved from an old ambulance, is used to admonish the crowds ahead to clear the way when their exuberance brings them out into the street.

Art Ryder Jr. serves as sound technician and, in a less glamorous capacity, as the number one "mule." (There are two other "mules," reserves, who take their turns.) It is the job of "the mule" to tow the whole rig by the boat-trailer tongue.

The ease with which the vehicle can be towed is one of its miracles. Art claims even a stiff wind can move it. He once went into an elaborate explanation of this phenomenon, but it was lost on me, a liberal arts major. I prefer to write it down as a miracle of delicate balance, a triumph over earthbound inertia.

What a joy, what a feeling of power, to poke one's clarinet, a mere twenty-eight inches of black tubing studded with metal keys, into one of those mics and flood the street with sound! You think as you play, *All that sound going out and up to the heavens is coming from me!* (The only such experience that has ever topped that one happened to me in the Louisiana Superdome when, at an international convention of travel agents, I heard the sound of my clarinet incredibly filling that cavernous structure as I played "Just a Closer Walk," with my good friend and great pianist Ronnie Kole and band solidly behind me.)

The "War Wagon" should be ranked in a supplementary listing of the "Wonders of the World." All who see it marvel at it. One of its greatest admirers is Gary Burghoff, "Radar" of M*A*S*H fame, an enthusiastic and capable jazz drummer, who walked and played with us Half-Fasters on a couple of Mardi Gras Days.

In 1989, as we began our rendezvous for what was to be my twenty-fourth walk with the Walking Club, I was surprised and a bit dismayed when I learned that the Wonderful Electric Sound Wagon was not to roll with us. Instead, Art's band was aboard a motor vehicle, actually riding! A couple of mics jutted out for the convenience of the walking players. I used one of the mics for the opening prayer. But it was not the same.

CHAPTER 8

The Mystery Chariot

*T*HE OTHER UNUSUAL VEHICLE THAT ROLLS with the Walking Club on Mardi Gras Day is, believe it or not, a chariot. It is no ordinary chariot and its primary purpose is unique in the history of chariots.

Necessity, it has been said wisely, is the mother of invention. The inventive mind of one of our Walking Club members conceived the idea of the chariot, and through his skill and industry it came to be. The necessity in question is the problem that vexes all paraders and spectators on Mardi Gras Day: How, with decency, does one answer when "nature calls"?

The obvious answer to this question, not altogether satisfactory, is scheduled rest stops. These we traditionally made. And then came the chariot.

The reason the rest stops presented a problem is, I think, fairly obvious. More than a hundred men have to stop, fall out of formation (I use the word very loosely!), file into the designated place – an office building, a lounge – queue up inside always-inadequate facilities, and wait their turn. Getting everybody back on the street at the prompting of many blasts of Wimpy's officious whistle is no small task. Eventually, we do get back together and resume our walk, as a few stragglers hurry to catch up. It is not an ideal arrangement. And so, enter the chariot.

The concept of the chariot and its execution were largely the work of one man, an officer in our Walking Club, Sal Diecidue. No one can actually pronounce Sal's surname correctly except Sal. Consequently, he is known to all as Sal "Dash."

A former business partner of Pete Fountain's, Sal owns and operates an ironworks business in New Orleans. He came to Pete with his idea of the chariot, left with Pete's blessing, and set to work.

Sal announced at a subsequent meeting of the Walking Club that he had begun to work on the solution to the problem. He refused to divulge the nature and *modus operandi* of the vehicle. When he asked the members for donations of pieces of discarded sheet metal, the mystery deepened. For weeks all that was known was that Sal was working on something on wheels that was the ultimate answer to the problem.

The chariot was constructed of sections of steel sheet metal welded together. The overall appearance of its body is that of a low-built, topless tank. It rolls on two wagon wheels that boast a distinctive pedigree. They were, half a century ago, on a float that was pulled by mules – as all the parade floats were at one time – and rolled proudly in the Rex parade on Mardi Gras Day.

On the tongue of the chariot there is the silhouette of a rearing black stallion. The tongue is attached to a beheaded van in which the valiant Leo Bowen and a few other non-walking members ride.

We still make rest stops, but fewer and shorter ones, because the chariot is the ongoing solution. One needs only to hop on from the open back end, proceed to the front of the chariot, assume a driver's position and stand in complete privacy (from the waist down). I trust it is not necessary to go into what Paul Harvey would call "the rest of the story."

Almost all of the members of the Walking Club agree with me that Sal's creation is an admirable solution to the problem. A few, however, are not entirely comfortable with it. This has puzzled me a bit and I have philosophized and theologized about it.

We poor mortals are part animal and part angel. It is the "angel" in us that we like to dwell on and cherish. We humans can love and laugh and sing. We can design and build skyscrapers, super-highways, ocean liners and jumbo jets. From the minds and hearts of humans flow great poetry, great music, great art. We probe the hidden world of microscopic life and reach out into the unlimited world of space.

Then there is that lumpy body of ours, with all its needs and limitations which keep us earthbound. Of itself, chemically speaking, mostly water with a few pounds of other chemicals blended in – calcium, potassium, phosphorus, magnesium, etc. That, and no more. The microscope of the biochemist can detect nothing else.

But man is not body only, nor is he spirit only. He is body *and* spirit or, better yet, body-spirit – a mystery of oneness from the hands of a loving, giving Creator.

I look at me, the totality of me. I reflect and I marvel. It strikes me that some people are ashamed of their bodies and bodily functions. I am all for modesty and physical decency, of course, because their opposites, for one thing, offend others. But that does not mean that I am ashamed of anything that my body is or does. I accept and respect myself as I am – "angel" and "animal," body and spirit. It is a package deal, a composite gift from a loving Creator.

"God don't make junk."

CHAPTER 9

My Roman Collar

B ACK IN THE SIXTIES, WHENEVER WE PRIESTS appeared in a public setting, we were expected to be in clerical dress, which includes the identifying Roman collar.

I conformed to that then and have continued to do so, even after Vatican II and on into the 1970s and '80s, when many have elected to discard the Roman collar altogether or wear it only on formal occasions. I have no quarrel with them. They have their reasons and I respect them. I have my reasons and I am sure they respect mine.

In any event, as I began to be identified as "The Jazz Priest," I decided early on to continue to show the traditional look of the Catholic priest. I certainly agree that "clothes don't make the man" – or the priest. In this day and age, when sensible people get to know you as a priest, you will stand or fall in their estimation because of who and what you are, not what you wear.

My decision to show up in traditional clerical garb in the

places where I play and listen to music was not a calculated one. I did not enter a process of prayer and discernment to arrive at it. It more or less happened that way. I just accepted clerical dress and have always been at peace with it. Besides, I am proud of my priesthood and I rather liked the idea of establishing that identity from the beginning, especially as I grew to view my jazz playing not only as exciting recreation but also as a ministry. And you have to be recognizable as a minister before you can minister.

I can assure you there are many souls out there in spiritual need who want to be helped – patrons, employees, musicians. Many do not know any priest or minister well enough to presume that taking their troubles to him is not an imposition. Furthermore, it is not easy to find the courage and determination to ring that rectory doorbell or, if one is Catholic, to go into that confessional.

*   *   *

"Got your horn with you, Father?"

"Just happen to have it with me."

"Come on up and play a couple of numbers with us, Father.... Let's have a good hand for Father Coco. He's a Jesuit priest. Where else but in New Orleans?"

The looks of curiosity, of incredulity, never cease to amuse me. I suspect they don't expect very much and are prepared to give polite applause. I once overheard some clear-cut skepticism as I passed the table of a group of beer-drinking Texans.

"What the hell is this?"

When I left the bandstand after playing a few numbers, I made a point of walking by their table. One man was generous in his compliments, so I struck up a conversation.

"Where are you from?" I asked.

"Midland, Texas."

"Don't you have anything like this in Midland, Texas?"

"Reverend, there ain't a damn thing in Midland, Texas."

"Except," I said, "a bunch of dirty old oil wells."

"Yeah, we got them all right."

I think I made a believer out of him, so to speak.

Speaking of ministry, I find it easy to read the mental process that sometimes brings patrons, employees and musicians to me with their fears, confusions and hurts. *Father is really human. Why, he plays jazz on the clarinet and really enjoys it. Seems like a regular fellow.* First, there is instant identification as a priest. Then, the drawbridge between me and them, in the form of the happy music that is jazz, drops, and they feel welcome to come across with their burdens and pains and heartaches.

I have had many opportunities to heal and help that would never have presented themselves were it not for my "jazz ministry."

Blessed be jazz!

A Sign Of Contradiction

*Y*ES, THE ROMAN COLLAR BRINGS INSTANT recognition. In public it attracts attention. It attracts people, some unpleasant, but mostly agreeable, friendly people.

It is, therefore, a biblical "sign of contradiction." That is the phrase Simeon used, as we read in Luke's gospel, when, in the presence of Mary and Joseph, he held the baby Jesus in his arms in the temple.

"You see this child: He is destined for the fall and rising of many in Israel... a sign of contradiction." (Luke 2:34)

The American flag, the hammer-and-sickle, a Masonic ring, a Knights of Columbus pin – all signs. They stand for something. People see them and react, and they can re-act in opposite, contradictory ways, depending on where they stand.

Jesus Christ was and is the supreme sign of contradiction. His cross was a sign of contradiction, and it still is. His mother and John and a few women stood on Calvary

in love and fidelity, while his enemies stood there taunt-
ing him and gloating. In our own century, George Ber-
nard Shaw let it be known that he wanted no "instrument
of execution" to be erected over his grave. On the other
hand, good Christians have died clutching the image of
their dying Lord.

And the Roman collar is, of course, a sign of contradiction. My most vivid negative recollection of that truth
goes back to an evening in The Blue Angel Club on Bourbon Street in New Orleans. The club featured excellent
Dixieland jazz.

I had never heard George Finola play. He was a cornetist out of Chicago, and I had heard high praise of him and
his band. When I learned that he was playing at The Blue
Angel, I decided to check him out. He proved to be an
outstanding jazzman.

But I got more than I bargained for that night.

I was alone, seated at a table right in front of the bandstand. As the music was in progress a woman walked by,
between me and the bandstand, and gave me (and my collar) an ugly look as she passed. She proceeded to the bar
and took a seat right at the end of the bar, near the bandstand. I wondered briefly about that look she gave me, but
put it out of my mind and became absorbed in the music.
In front of me were a tall glass of ice water and a Scotch-
on-the-rocks.

Thirty minutes or so later, she again walked by my
table on her way out. This time, however, she paused for
an instant, turned her head in my direction and glared at
me (and my Roman collar). With a flip of the back of her
hand, she tipped over the glass of water, spilling its con-
tents into my lap. Hardly breaking stride, she walked out
of the club and onto Bourbon Street.

An alert waiter, who saw me dabbing frantically with
napkin and handkerchief, came quickly with a towel.

"Did you see that?" I asked.

"See what, Father?"

"What that woman did, the one who was sitting at the end of the bar? She deliberately knocked that glass of water over into my lap."

"I saw her, but I didn't see that happen."

"Well, it was no accident, I can tell you that."

Surprisingly, I was not angry, but I was baffled and dismayed. What demon would possess a person – whom I had never seen before and who had never seen me before – to do such a thing? What put that kind of venom in her veins? Obviously, the Roman collar was a sign to her, a sign of the Church, of the Catholic priesthood. What evil had happened in her past? What priest had offended her? What nun had hurt her? What teaching or practice of the Catholic Church was galling her?

My friend, Carlo Montalbano – owner of The Blue Angel and gracious host of our Walking Club every year on one of our rest stops at his club – hurried over to my table.

"They told me what happened. I'm sorry about that, Father. I know who she is. She comes in here a lot. A go-go dancer out of work. She drinks too much. I guarantee you that'll never happen again. She'll never come back in my place again."

"No, no," I said. "It's okay. I feel sorry for somebody who would do a thing like that. Why would a person want to do something like that? I'd like to know. Something must have happened to her. I wonder what it was?"

I was saddened that night, and whenever I recall that incident it still saddens me. I suppose I should have followed her out and tried to talk to her, to communicate. Perhaps I could have helped her. It seemed so impractical an idea at the time. It seems reasonable today. Perhaps I just lacked the moral courage, rationalized, and so missed an opportunity to reach out and heal.

Most of the negative responses to the Roman collar in

the French Quarter, and like places of entertainment, can be irksome but are generally relatively insignificant. I recall some incidents from the past. For instance, the female voice coming out of a passing car, beginning a mock confession: "Bless me, Father, for I have sinned." Or that man on the street, too tipsy to talk sense, but who wanted to talk. As I began to disengage myself, he said he was Jewish and that is why I did not want to talk to him, that I did not like Jews.

"No, I love Jews. My boss is Jewish. His name is Jesus Christ," I told him.

A number of such encounters – far, far fewer than the many pleasant encounters I have had through the years – have occurred. They present no real problem. The sad memory of that go-go dancer, however, still comes back to haunt me from time to time.

CHAPTER 11

To New York City Via Clarinet

*T*HROUGH THE YEARS MY CLARINET HAS opened many doors for me and at times has catapulted me to faraway places.

Each year it sends me flying to Tampa, Florida, for what I like to call an expenses-paid mini-vacation. I play there at Jesuit High School's annual benefit, called "A Night to Remember." Two of the most memorable trips my clarinet has won for me were to New York City and Los Angeles.

I was at Our Lady of the Oaks Retreat House in Grand Coteau, Louisiana, where I was stationed from 1971 to 1976 and to which I returned in 1982.

One day during the latter stay I received a phone call from New Orleans. The caller was a representative of Eastern Airlines, the regional director, I believe. My friend, pianist Ronnie Kole, had suggested that he phone me. Ronnie's trio was to play at a benefit in New Orleans sponsored in part by Eastern.

Would I be willing to play? I checked my schedule. No

conflicts. When? Where? What? As ever, I was eager to oblige.

The event was a formal dinner at Antoine's. The purpose was to raise funds for a medical center in Atlanta. The occasion was the inaugural flight of a new-model plane being added to Eastern's fleet.

A planeload of donors flew into New Orleans from Atlanta in the late afternoon. They were bussed to Antoine's for the private event – a cocktail party followed by a lavish gourmet dinner. We provided the music. After dinner there was impromptu dancing. Late that night the reluctant revellers were bussed back to Moisant Airport for the return flight to Atlanta.

I had been reassured that I would receive a check to cover my travel expenses – reward enough for me anytime – but did not anticipate the surprising bonus: a roundtrip ticket to any city in the continental United States to which Eastern flies. I chose New York City, never having visited there previously.

I have a nephew, one of my brother's sons, who lives in lower Manhattan and is a faculty member at Columbia University's graduate school of drama. Bill Coco is a bachelor. With a roundtrip ticket, a place to stay and a relative who knew his way around New York City and who happened not to be teaching that summer, I had it made.

Some delightful musical happenings came my way during the five or six days I spent there. I fell in love with The Big Apple.

With hope in my heart, I had brought along my clarinet, just in case. Several opportunities to sit in did present themselves, with a little self-promotion and the help of a friend, the fine young clarinetist Rick Hardeman, whom I had come to know in New Orleans. He was now performing in New York.

Rick and his wife Elaine and I had dinner at a Japanese restaurant within walking distance of two famous Dixieland clubs. Dixieland jazz was not easy to find in New York City, but we did find Eddie Condon's and Jimmy Ryan's. Rick spoke up for me at both places, and I was invited to sit in at one and turned down at the other. The presence of a jazz clarinet player in clerical garb elicited some interesting reaction.

At Ryan's I met an agreeable young drummer, the son of the late, great trumpet player Bobby Hackett. I was able to tell him that I once sat in with his dad's combo at a Bourbon Street lounge in the late sixties.

While in New York City, I had the pleasure of sitting in with a remarkable jazz guitarist, Bucky Pizzarelli, who had worked with Benny Goodman. Bucky had performed in New Orleans at the Hyatt Regency, which is where I met him. I had sat in with his group.

Now Bucky was appearing at the swanky Café Pierre in the Hotel Pierre in New York. I sat in the hotel's lobby near the entrance to the cafe, wondering before Bucky showed up if he would remember me. He did remember me and immediately began asking about musicians whom he had met in New Orleans, among them a thunderous, capable jazz drummer named Freddie Kohlman, who now had a club in New York City.

"I came to catch your show," I said. "And I have my horn with me. I don't know if you care to let people sit in…"

"Sure," Bucky said. "Just let us do the first set. Dinner music, you know. Then we'll swing, have some fun."

And swing we did! And fun we had! It was an exciting evening.

I also got to play at Freddie Kohlman's place for what was called "Jazz in the Afternoon." I had heard about this gig from a lady travel agent from New York who was attending a convention in New Orleans some years earlier. She explained the event was held on Fridays from 11 a.m. to 2 p.m. Its distinctive feature was that the participants were not professional musicians, but came from other professions and every walk of life. The leader was, I believe, in the advertising business, a very capable alto saxophone player. A trombonist was an Episcopal priest. One of the drummers happened to be no less than head of the Cardiology Department of Mt. Sinai Hospital. They had one thing in common: They all loved jazz and could play with varying degrees of ability. Some were mediocre; some were good; some were great.

It was a Thursday afternoon when I phoned Freddie's and learned that there would be a session the following day. I was given the name of the leader of the program, the alto sax player, and I tracked him down by phone.

He was very cordial. I introduced myself and gave him my credentials. He sounded interested and said I would be most welcome.

It was an afternoon to remember. I felt right at home from the very beginning. The Roman collar didn't seem to affect anyone unduly.

My alto sax man was well in control, but the program flowed with a minimum of organization, delightfully relaxed and informal. As always at such happenings, there were professional musicians present, not to play but to listen and be where the action was. One invited me to sit in with his band that evening, an invitation I had to decline with regret.

Two pros, however, did play that afternoon at Freddie's: a vibraphonist and a guitarist, both impressive musicians. I was, to use a Southern expression, "in high cotton."

"Don't worry, New York City; I'll be back."

I don't know who penned those amusing words, but that is a promise I'd love to make and keep.

CHAPTER 12

To Los Angeles Via Clarinet

ONE OF MY FAVORITE BANDS IS BANU Gibson's Red Hot Jazz Band. Off the bandstand Banu is Mrs. Bruce Podewell, mother of two, whose husband is a member of the Tulane University faculty and a good musician in his own right.

On the bandstand she is the bandleader, a potent little package of entertainment: quick-witted emcee with a facile rapport with her audience, solid banjoist and guitarist and, above all, a singer with a wonderfully big voice that comes miraculously out of her petite, bouncy body.

Banu's instrumentation usually consists of a piano, bass, drums, trumpet (or cornet) and trombone – but no reed instrument. So, she is always glad to see me show up with my clarinet to bring the band up to Dixieland strength.

I have spent many pleasant evenings listening to and sitting in with her sharp little combo. On one such evening I came into a free trip to Los Angeles.

It was mid-summer in the Court Tavern, the lounge of

The Court of Two Sisters. This French Quarter restaurant with two entrances, one on Royal Street and the other on Bourbon Street, has as lovely a patio as you will see anywhere. The lounge is one step off Bourbon Street, and its front door is left open for the edification of the passersby.

Jim McNelley, whom I had never met or even seen before, stopped, looked in, liked what he was seeing and hearing, and came in. I happened to be on the bandstand doing my usual two or three solos per set. I bowed to the applause, left the bandstand, and sat down. I was sitting alone, as was often the case. Jim came to my table.

"Do you mind if I sit with you?" Jim asked.

"Not at all. I'm by myself."

"Are you really a priest?"

I pointed to my Roman collar.

"Yes. This is for real. Jazz is my hobby. I have an open invitation to sit in with any number of bands in this area."

"I think you missed your calling," Jim offered.

I hear that often, and I have a standard answer.

"No, I have two callings, jazz and the priesthood."

Sometimes I add my standing one-liner:

"I'm a jazz musician but I moonlight as a priest."

"I've been up and down the street," Jim said. "This is the best band I've heard. I'd like to hire this band. Do you think they would go all the way to L.A. for one night?"

"They'd go anywhere for one night if the price is right," I replied.

He proceeded to tell me he was the director of Riverside Community Hospital in Riverside, California. He said he had come to Houston to attend a convention, and, never having been to New Orleans, decided to rent a car and drive over.

"Every two years," Jim continued, "we have what we call Awards and Appreciation Night. Doctors, nurses, employees

I entered the Society of Jesus at Grand Coteau, La., in the summer of 1938, and I made my first vows two years later. This photo was taken near that time.

My sister, Rose Rita Coco, and I pose for a picture outside our home in Helena, Arkansas, circa 1937-38, shortly before I left for the Jesuit novitiate. She later was named Sr. Rita Maria when she joined a religious order, the Sisters of Charity of Nazareth (Nazareth, Kentucky).

Our big, Catholic Sicilian family was made up of eleven members. I went home to Arkansas for the first time in ten years, in 1948, and we all got together for a family portrait. First row, seated left to right, are: me; my mother, Giovannina Santo Colombo Coco; my father, Rosario Coco; and my sister, now called Sr. Rita Maria of the Sisters of Charity of Nazareth. My other siblings, on the second row, left to right, are: Sarah, Vincent, Sam, Jimmy, Joe, Mary and Anthony, who became a Jesuit brother.

That's me on the left showing John Hein, one of my colleagues from the Jesuit novitiate, how to cook meatballs and spaghetti. The picture was taken in St. Marys, Kansas, in 1950. The recipe was handed down to me by my mother, a great Italian cook, who was born and reared in Cefalu, Sicily, the same hometown as my father.

Though the clarinet is the instrument I have used most in my musical career, I also developed some proficiency with the saxophone. That's me in the black cassock, practicing for a performance sometime in the mid-1960s.

I spent quite a number of years (32 in all) as a retreat director at both Jesuit-run retreat houses in south Louisiana – Our Lady of the Oaks at Grand Coteau (above) and Manresa House of Retreats in Convent (facing page). Both facilities are beautiful, peaceful and conducive to heartfelt prayer and contemplation. The retreats are refreshing to the human spirit; they are based on the Spiritual Exercises of St. Ignatius, the founder of the Jesuit Order.

My clarinet and my old Sears typewriter are the tools of the trade for a guy who enjoys playing jazz music and writing. This is the clarinet I used on numerous occasions while performing in New Orleans nightclubs, and the typewriter I used to write my book, Blessed Be Jazz. *By the way, most of the book was written in 1987 and 1988 while I was on sabbatical leave, which I spent at Weston Jesuit School of Theology in Cambridge, Mass.*

– everybody associated in any way with the hospital – are invited to a supper dance. We have speeches, awards, about 500 hospital people and each can bring one guest. So there will be about 1,000 people. We have it in the city auditorium. I'd like to hire this band for the occasion. It's next spring."

"Talk to Banu's manager," I suggested. "He's the trombone player."

"Will you come with the band and play, Father?"

"Well, let me put it this way: I'm entitled to a couple of weeks of vacation, and I've never been to California. If you can give me enough notice, I can plan on going. If I do go, I'd like to spend a week or so. I'm not a professional musician. I don't play for money, but if you pay my airfare, it's a deal."

"I can do better than that. Leave your wallet at home. You'll be my guest," he said.

I gave him my address and my phone number.

Jim McNelley had a gleam in his eye. He was already planning the affair.

"We'll surprise 'em. You'll be in the audience, and I'll say, 'I want you to meet a friend of mine in the audience.' Then I'll ask you to come up on the stage, and then we'll surprise 'em."

The band was eventually booked. They settled on a Thursday in March, since the auditorium was not available on the weekend.

Well before the date, I received in the mail a roundtrip plane ticket to L.A., on Delta Airlines. I flew in on a Monday and took a cab to Loyola-Marymount University, a Jesuit institution, to spend the first couple of days in residence with my fellow Jesuits.

I was able to get around and see some of the sights, thanks to a young man whom I had met in New Orleans some years earlier. His name is Mian, and he was a gemologist in Beverly Hills.

It was jazz that brought us together. We met when I was sitting in with a fine Dixieland band, The New Dukes of Dixieland, in the Dukes' Place, a lounge atop the Hotel Monteleone in the French Quarter. I noticed the guy, in his early thirties, dark and handsome, responding enthusiastically to the music. I surmised that he was from the Near East, but later learned he was from Pakistan. He had come to the United States as a teenager, found employment at a New Orleans motel, and later moved out to the West Coast. He became a gemologist and eventually co-owner of one of the most prestigious jewelry stores in California, located on the fabled Rodeo Drive in Beverly Hills.

The night we met he was beaming like one of his diamonds.

"I heard you play at the Maison Bourbon once," he said. "Here's my card. If you ever get out to L.A., look me up."

He handed me a very flashy business card.

"I'm not very likely to get out to L.A., but if I do, I will," I said.

I kept the card. I have a small case full of business cards received in places where I have played through the years, each annotated with the month, year and place.

Before I left for L.A. I fished out that card and put it in my wallet.

Jazz brings together the most unlikely people. He, a Pakistani Muslim and gemologist, and I, a Roman Catholic priest and clarinet-playing Jesuit from Arkansas.

Mian was the soul of warm hospitality. We shared a couple of meals, conversed about jazz, religion and jewelry. I spent some time in his place of business, inspecting expensive jewelry, learning something about the inner workings and tight security of a Rodeo Drive jewelry store. His chief security officer, a former member of the L.A. police force, took me on a private tour of his old beat in Beverly Hills.

The third day of my stay was spent at the beautiful Jesuit retreat house, named Manresa, like her sister retreat facility in Louisiana. I remember best the profusion of gorgeous flowers all around the place and the genial hospitality of the California Jesuits. I enjoyed spending time with the only family of which I am a member, the worldwide family of the Society of Jesus, the Jesuits.

Thursday morning Jim McNelley drove from Riverside to Azusa, where the retreat house is located, to pick me up. We made a couple of interesting stops on the way, one at a small winery. A bottle of excellent sherry found its way into my suitcase, one of many kindnesses of my host. Jim proudly assured me that one could not purchase this particular vintage anywhere but in California.

When we arrived in Riverside he drove me to the Holiday Inn. The members of Banu Gibson's Red Hot Jazz Band were there, having just arrived from New Orleans. We all went to lunch at a venerable hotel, whose faded glory was being restored. I recall inspecting in the lobby an enormous chair, custom-built for a distinguished former guest of enormous girth, President William Howard Taft. It seems to me I was told that Richard Nixon and his bride honeymooned here, as well.

The party that night was a rousing success. The theme of the evening was "New Orleans Mardi Gras." They loved every minute of it. They loved the Dixieland music, the world's happiest music. They loved the banners and bunting festooning the walls and ceiling in the purple, green and gold of Mardi Gras. There were a king and a queen of the evening, in true Mardi Gras style. There was a mock Mardi Gras parade that snaked its way around the hall, complete with second-lining, spinning umbrellas and flying doubloons. The consensus: "The greatest party we ever had."

The weekend that rounded off my visit to L.A. was most enjoyable. Jim McNelley was a solicitous host, an expert tour guide, and a courageous and efficient driver in the competitive setting of the mazy L.A. freeways.

Jim was divorced and lived with his teenage son, a mature and thoughtful youngster, in a little house in San Juan Capistrano, forty or so miles from his workplace in Riverside.

We spent the better part of Saturday at Disneyland, marvelling at the outgrowth of one of the most creative imaginations with which God ever graced humankind.

Shortly before I left New Orleans, I had learned that Banu had starred as a singer and actress for seven years in Disneyland's famed "Horseshoe Revue." Now she was backstage, visiting with the cast, many of them former associates, as we stood in line outside, waiting to see this much-touted show.

The show, Gay Nineties style, was great fun. In one of its highlights, a girl leaves the stage and wanders among the tables to flirt brazenly with the male patrons. Banu had set us up. I smiled when the flirt inevitably made her way to our table. I laughed when she planted a kiss on the top of Jim's bald dome, leaving the red smudge of lipstick.

"What are *you* laughing at, Big Boy?"

She turned to me. It was entrapment, pure and simple. I could see Banu's hand in this and guessed that she might be peeking from backstage and enjoying our brief notoriety. She was.

The J. Paul Getty Museum, Santa Monica Beach and the majesty of the Pacific, the old Franciscan Mission (where I was moved as I concelebrated Sunday Mass) – all of it made for a memorable weekend.

Banu and her band were still in town. She had booked into a lounge, one of her old haunts, on the Friday evening and Sunday afternoon. She still had a following out there. I rejoined them, sat in with the band for a couple of numbers, met some local musicians who gravitated toward the place, then returned to Loyola-Marymount that evening.

All in all, it was an eventful week, thanks be to jazz – and to Jim McNelley. I had one small regret when I left and headed home to New Orleans and Grand Coteau: I had missed the return of the swallows to Capistrano by only a few days.

CHAPTER 13

One of My 'Big Three'

OF ALL THE NEW ORLEANS MUSICIANS WITH whom I have had the privilege of playing, the most famous, by far, are Pete Fountain and Al Hirt. They are nationally and even internationally known. To this pair I would add Ronnie Kole and call them my "Big Three."

The fame Pete and Al have achieved has eluded Ronnie, and I cannot fathom why, for Ronnie is such a superb pianist.

I first heard The Ronnie Kole Trio in 1966 in an open-air concert in New Orleans' City Park Stadium – a relic of the Depression era that is used largely for high school athletic contests. The event was a police benefit show to raise funds, if I remember correctly, for widows of policemen and their families.

My brother Sam, his wife and one of their daughters were on vacation in New Orleans. We went to the show to hear the two stars in the program, Pete Fountain and Al Hirt. To us at the time, Ronnie Kole was just another name on the program.

Pete and Al performed admirably, and the crowd responded wildly. When The Ronnie Kole Trio was introduced I had no idea what to expect. *What kind of impact,* I thought, *could a piano, backed by bass and drums, make in an open-air setting, in a football stadium?*

I did not expect much. But when Ronnie pounded out those opening chords and the bass and drums followed him into his first number, I was overwhelmed. It was love at first hearing.

The images that come to me when I experience the finesse and power of Ronnie Kole's playing are the hands of a master surgeon and the arms of a blacksmith – delicacy and strength.

I decided that night that I must meet this man, and I must hear him and his Trio play in a small and more congenial setting. I did so one evening at a time when he was appearing nightly at the Court Tavern in the Court of Two Sisters in the French Quarter.

Ronnie is a native of Chicago, as is Richard Taylor, the drummer in the Trio. Everett Link, the bassist, is a New Orleanian. I have remained close to both Richard and Everett, who are among the best in their field, through the years. Everett Link is an exemplary Catholic. Our association (again, thanks be to jazz) led later to my becoming his confessor and spiritual director. Everett and his wife Barbara are active in youth work in their parish.

That eventful night at the Court Tavern marked the beginning of a long and rich relationship. After the first set, I introduced myself. Ronnie was warm and cordial. He had heard of my association with Pete Fountain's Walking Club and that I was something of a musician. Not being able to stay the whole evening, I had to leave during a late set. I called for my check and was told by the waitress, "Mr. Kole will take care of it."

My first opportunity to sit in with Ronnie Kole mis-fired.

The Trio had played before a good crowd till the end of the evening, but a number of people stayed on and were asking for more.

"I can't keep my guys overtime. They're tired. But I'll take a little break and come back and play for you," Ronnie said.

He turned to me.

"Staying, Father?"

I nodded.

"Got your horn with you?"

My heart sank to the soles of my feet. I shook my head.

"No, it's at home."

But there were other occasions later, many of them during the years that followed, to taste the excitement of sitting in with a true master, in a dozen different clubs in the New Orleans area. There was to be also a succession of conventions and benefit appearances in Louisiana, as well as a few in Texas and Mississippi. One opportunity, in Arkansas, was the highlight of it all: a concert in Helena, my hometown.

There was a gentleman farmer, a bachelor, whose name was Warfield, who had lived and died in Helena. He left a small fortune to be invested, and directed that the revenue accruing from the investment be used to underwrite free concerts and other cultural events for the citizens of Helena and its environs. In November of 1975 the Warfield Foundation sponsored The Ronnie Kole Trio in concert, featuring me, a native son, as guest soloist.

It was a proud moment for my family and friends when I stepped onto the stage and under the spotlight in the Lily Peters Auditorium of Phillips County Junior College that evening. Warm waves of nostalgia washed over my soul. It was to be my first hometown public appearance since I left home at the age of seventeen, thirty-seven years earlier. What a homecoming!

If my return to Helena was a big event in my life, so was the making of the first album containing my work. Released in 1978, it was an album of clarinet and tenor saxophone solos, titled "A Closer Walk with Three." It included six clarinet and three tenor sax solos, featuring my clarinet version of "Just a Closer Walk with Thee."

"Closer Walk" is surely New Orleans' most loved gospel song. In the liner notes of the album, I wrote:

"Pete Fountain owns that number. I have only borrowed it for limited use."

The way this album came about was not a matter of careful and elaborate planning. It more or less just happened. It came out of the many numbers I played with The Ronnie Kole Trio on many different occasions. Ronnie was often asked:

"Do you have an album with Father Coco on it?"

"No, but we're going to cut one some day," he'd respond.

I considered this reply nothing more than polite rhetoric. But one evening, in that way Ronnie Kole has of rushing to a decision, he said to me:

"Let's make that album. Draw up a list of fifteen or twenty numbers we've been doing. Then we'll sit down and pick out some, maybe ten or so."

So, one morning I drove to his home in Slidell, La., bringing along my clarinet, tenor sax and a list of numbers. The two of us sat down after lunch and went to work.

During the afternoon we settled on ten numbers: "Closer Walk," "Margie," "Mood Indigo," "Blue Prelude," "Hello, Dolly," and "*Bei Mir Bist Du Schoen*" on clarinet; and "Love Theme from The Godfather," "Charade," "Who's Sorry Now?" and "Shangri-La" on tenor sax.

We recorded all ten on the original tape, but later scrubbed "Shangri-La" because Ronnie was dissatisfied with his part on it.

Two days later, Ronnie, Everett, Richard and I met in

Ronnie's private studio in Slidell and recorded the album in one afternoon. Ronnie played on a Fender Rhodes (a small electric piano) that afternoon, simply chording behind my solos and playing the simple melody on his solo spots. Later he overdubbed his own brilliant grand piano solos. Effectively, one is listening to five instrumentalists, including Ronnie and Ronnie. On Ronnie's solos the simultaneity of theme (on the Fender Rhodes) and improvisations was a happy accident.

We stumbled on the album's title, "A Closer Walk with Three," quite casually. A member of one of our audiences produced it spontaneously one evening.

The Trio and I were playing for our good friend Fr. Richard Carroll, pastor of St. Margaret Mary Church in Slidell, at one of his "Meet the New Parishioners" gatherings. Ronnie informed the listeners that the Trio and I were planning to cut a record in the near future. He would add that we were searching for a good title and, tongue-in-cheek, sought their reaction to "The Saint and the Sinner" or "Coco-Kole Ah!" as titles.

The latter title, offered by an inventive acquaintance of mine in Opelousas, La., Charles Lanusse, inevitably elicited groans from the audience. Charles had even gone so far as to sketch an album cover featuring a Coke bottle and suggested we ask the Coca-Cola company to pay for the endorsement!

Someone in the audience spoke up after we had finished doing "Closer Walk."

"How about 'A Closer Walk with *Three*?' – Father Coco and the Trio?"

Ronnie and I looked at one another. We both smiled and nodded agreement.

"Not bad," said Ronnie, "not bad at all."

We had a title.

After many years together, these three splendid musicians went their separate musical ways. They continue to perform in the New Orleans area but no longer as a unit. It is always a pleasure for me to encounter any one of them wherever and with whomever he may be playing. And I know I am always welcome to sit in.

But sometimes the joy of resuming my "closer walk" with them in music and friendship is tinged with a touch of sadness, because the Ronnie Kole Trio that was my first love, and with whom I spent so many happy hours, is now only a memory, albeit one of my fondest.

CHAPTER 14

Death on the Dance Floor

*A*S I'VE STATED PREVIOUSLY, THE GREAT majority of my experiences in the world of jazz have been pleasant, many of them deeply rewarding. But a few have been unpleasant, and one was downright shocking.

A remark I made in one of those unpleasant occurrences proved to be a prophesy of a tragic event that would come to pass a few years later.

An unpleasant incident occurred at Charley's Corner, an attractive little lounge in the Chateau Lemoyne, a motel in the French Quarter on Dauphine and Bienville Streets. The Ronnie Kole Trio was appearing there nightly; I would go by frequently to listen, learn and sit in.

One evening after I had done my stint as guest soloist, I was sitting at my table. Bass player Everett Link had joined me. Right next to us sat a middle-aged man who was directing a blank stare at me. I could not guess what was on his mind, but it was clear that he was not happy. I tried to ignore him, until he addressed me directly.

"I don't think what you're doing is right," he said.

His speech was slurred. He had obviously had one (or more) too many.

"I just don't think a Catholic priest ought to be playing jazz in a lounge."

There's that pre-fab image of a priest again.

"Why not?"

"Well, am I allowed to commit adultery?"

"I don't follow you," I said. "Adultery is sinful. It's against the law of God. It's against one of the Ten Commandments. 'Thou shalt not commit adultery.' There's no commandment I know of that says, 'Thou shalt not play jazz in a lounge if thou art a priest.'"

"Suppose I had a heart attack or something and needed a priest, and you're up there playing jazz."

The man specialized in *non sequiturs*.

Then Everett Link jumped into the discussion.

"You'd be lucky. Father would be here," he observed.

A cocktail waitress, who up to this point had been an interested bystander, entered the fray to defend me. She began quoting the Bible to him.

"If you had a heart attack while I was on the bandstand," I added, "I assure you, as much as I love to play, I would stop in the middle of a solo and minister to you."

At this, the poor fellow got up angrily and left. And I wondered what kind of venom was stirring inside him. And what had poisoned his spirit.

Several years after this incident, my prophecy was fulfilled when I did stop in the middle of a solo to minister to the victim of a heart attack. It was on a Sunday night at the Jefferson-Orleans North, an admirable facility owned and operated by bandleader Pat Barberot.

Pat leads one of the top big swing bands in the city – in the state, for that matter. His Jefferson-Orleans North hosts wedding receptions and various kinds of meetings and convocations, and, above all, it is one of the most popular ballrooms in the area. The annual Christmas dance of Pete Fountain's Walking Club takes place there, and you can look for Pete to play some guest solos with Pat's band backing him at these dances. I have been known to do the same.

At the Jefferson-Orleans North there is a popular Sunday institution, Singles' Night, a dance that runs from 7 p.m. to 11:00 p.m. It is well-attended, largely by the unattached seeking a place for an evening of entertainment with decency and dignity. Most of the dancers are regulars and have come to know one another well through the years.

Betty, who was divorced, was one of those regulars. She was well-liked by those who frequented these weekly reunions. She was on the dance floor the first Sunday night I sat in with the band.

I was in the middle of a solo, playing "Just a Closer Walk with Thee," when there came a commotion on the dance floor. I heard panicky voices. I looked up to see dancers standing around someone who had fallen. We stopped playing. Someone came to the bandstand and summoned me.

"Father, I think you'd better come."

I hopped off the bandstand and pushed my way through the crowd. Betty was stretched out on the floor. One of Pat's men was on a walkie-talkie calling for a rescue unit. Two men were on the floor, on their knees alongside her, administering C.P.R.

"Is she Catholic?" I asked.

"Yes," someone said.

I knelt beside her, leaned forward, lips close to her ear. "This is Fr. Coco. Can you hear me?"

The two men continued, one pounding her chest, the other giving mouth-to-mouth resuscitation.

"Can you hear me, Betty?"

I put her hand in mine. It was cold.

"Squeeze my hand if you understand me. Can you hear

me?"

No response.

Lips closer to her ear, I began to recite the Act of Contrition. I ad-libbed other prayers.

Then, the paramedics arrived and took over. As they were preparing to take her to the emergency room of nearby East Jefferson Hospital, I returned to the bandstand.

Pat Barberot was in a quandary. Should the dance be continued? Or should it be terminated?

"What do you think we ought to do, Father?" He was shaken.

"I think you ought to continue," I said. "I don't think Betty would want you to stop, if she had her say. You want me to say something?"

"Would you?"

He was clearly relieved.

I stepped up to the mic.

"May I have your attention, please? May I have your attention?"

A hush quickly fell over the dance floor, and the dancers, who had been milling around, stopped in their tracks and looked toward the bandstand.

"We're not sure how Betty is, but it doesn't look good. Probably a heart attack. But Betty loved to dance, and I don't think she would want you to stop because of her. I'm sure she would want you to continue."

The band resumed playing as I left the hall to drive to the hospital. When I arrived I took my sick-call kit from the glove compartment and hurried to the emergency room, where I was told she had already been pronounced dead.

I went into the cubicle where her sheet-shrouded body lay. I uncovered her face, anointed her forehead with sacramental oil, and read the appropriate prayers from my ritual.

Since she had already been pronounced dead, was my

action a meaningless gesture, an exercise in futility?

Officially, clinically, Betty was dead. But death is a mystery, and who can define it? A scientist would say that the inert form under that sheet was now nothing more than an aggregate of a dozen or so chemicals. And he would be right. But is clinical death absolute death?

Beneath that white sheet lay an intricate marvel of God's creative design. The spirit of Betty had, just a couple of hours before, informed it, animated it. So recently it was one with the person of Betty, smiling, laughing, dancing. Where was that spirit now? What's its relationship to that still form? Who can tell?

So, I anointed her, tracing the form of the cross on her forehead with an oil-smeared thumb that she could not feel and reciting prayers which she could not hear. I did so in the hope that what these actions symbolize – the healing touch and merciful voice of Jesus Christ – might reach the spirit of the person who began her journey of faith anointed with the oil of Baptism and was now continuing on that journey toward the full embrace of God.

CHAPTER 15

'Jumbo' and I

I FIRST HEARD THE GREAT TRUMPET PLAYER
Al Hirt – "Jumbo," to his friends and acquaintances
– in the summer of 1952. Al was about thirty at that time
and had not achieved the international fame that is his today.

The occasion was a show, a spectacular array of musical talent, in the quadrangle of Loyola University of the
South, in New Orleans. Most, if not all, of the singers and
other musicians were students or alumnae and alumni of
the Loyola School of Music.

"A Night Under The Stars," or some such title, was the
way the show was billed. I was at Loyola that summer to
teach a course in theology, having just completed my own
theological studies.

It was a sultry summer, but otherwise one of the most
enjoyable summers of my Jesuit life. I had come from
four years of "exile" in St. Marys, Kansas, a far cry from
the south Louisiana I had left and come to love. It was in

eastern Kansas that I pursued my theological studies and was ordained to the priesthood. I welcomed the news that, after my final exams, I was to return to the city I loved, where I had taught (at Jesuit High School) during my pre-priesthood days, from 1945 to 1948.

I can remember well the last leg of my train trip back South, sitting in a coach of the old Panama Limited out of Memphis, watching the Mississippi and then the Louisiana landscape flying by, knowing that I was headed to my beloved New Orleans, but only for the summer. At summer's end I was scheduled to begin the final months of my Jesuit training at Xavier Hall in Pass Christian, Miss., but what and where my long-term future would be after that, I had no way of knowing.

It was a hot, glorious summer, and one of its glories was that night under the stars in the Loyola quadrangle. It was there that I saw a hulk of a man, build like an NFL noseguard, amble out onto the stage with a trumpet under his arm. He reached the mic, put his trumpet to his lips, jiggled the keys a bit and, on cue, let fly.

I was astonished at what I heard, spell-bound. We are all hero-worshipers to some degree. My heroes and heroines are musicians, writers and athletes. (Jesus Christ and the saints, canonized and uncanonized, belong in the category of the superheroic.) That night Al Hirt was enrolled in my personal Musicians' Hall of Fame.

The prospect of hearing him again somewhere was a pleasant thought. Appearing on the same program with him was far from my thoughts that summer night. But appear with him I did about three years later, on the stage of the Jesuit High auditorium in New Orleans. It was to Jesuit High School that I was eventually assigned, and my gig with Al Hirt happened in the first of the sixteen successive years I taught there as a priest.

Most of our schools conduct an annual "mission drive" to raise funds for the foreign missions staffed by Jesuits.

At Jesuit High of New Orleans, it occurred in the second semester, during the Lenten season. There was interclass competition, which inspired varied and sometimes ingenious schemes for raising money. One year I taught a senior class whose president was Pat Screen – LSU football star of the 1960s and later the mayor of Baton Rouge – that netted a goodly sum of money by person-to-person sales of quarts of Perfecto brand olives. Pat was my most successful salesman. There were rummage sales, cake sales, crawfish boils.

In that first year someone conceived the idea of a faculty talent night to raise funds for the missions. To shore up the evening's entertainment we added a professional bonus in the form of The Dawnbusters, a combo featuring the trumpet of Al Hirt; also performing was one of my favorite musicians, who later played vibes beautifully for many years with Pete Fountain, Godfrey Hirsch. The Dawnbusters were doing live broadcasts over WWL radio in those days. And that is how I happened to meet Al Hirt and appear on the same program with him.

Some of the faculty members at Jesuit High had negative feeling about the idea of a faculty talent night, fearing that exposing our talents, such as they were, to an auditorium full of students could be disastrous. But bolder heads prevailed, and the show went on.

The show went well. The boys, predictably, proved to be a lively audience (to say the least). You could tell whether they liked or disliked your performance. They communicated.

I chose to play the saxophone that night because my playing was rusty at that time and the sax is easier to manage than the clarinet, my favored instrument. I was backed by two young Jesuits on bass and piano. The boys received us well, and a smile and approving nod from Al Hirt made my night.

The opportunity to sit in and play with Al Hirt's own

band came my way some twenty years later. It came as a result of an invocation that I delivered at a testimonial banquet honoring him. November 26, 1975 was proclaimed by the mayor of New Orleans "Al Hirt Day." The city was honoring one of her now-famous sons. A dear friend, Tony Benedetto, faithful Manresa retreatant (where I met him), then-president of the New Orleans Jazz Club, suggested that I be invited to deliver the invocation at the banquet. The invitation was extended, and I accepted.

In that invocation, I spoke of our honoree's "steel chops" and "flying fingers." The phrase that I liked, as did Al, referred to him as a "bearded, earth-bound Gabriel." When I finished reading the invocation, hand-printed on parchment in fine Gothic script by a nun friend of mine, I walked up to Al and presented it to him.

"This is really nice, Father. Thank You," Al said.

"Wait a minute now," I said. "This is going to cost you something."

"How much?"

"I don't mean money. I'm coming to your club, and the price is to sit in with your band and play a couple of numbers."

"You got it," Al agreed.

I think it was the following night that I showed up at Al Hirt's Bourbon Street club, horn in hand, well before the 10:30 p.m. starting time. I sent word to Al backstage that I was in the audience and had come "to collect."

Promptly at 10:30 the band, minus Al Hirt, began to play a warm-up number. Little Pee Wee (God rest his talented soul!) was wailing away on clarinet; Jim Black, solid and steady Texan, on bass; bulky Joe Prejean, a virtual musical gymnast, on trombone; loveable, driving little Paul "Mouse" Ferrara on drums; on piano, sophisticated and elegant artist, Ronnie Dupont. A number of other outstanding musicians played in other Al Hirt bands, but this combo was my all-time favorite. I suppose it was because there is no love like first love. That night was for me the first of many exciting nights in Al Hirt's club, to listen and to sit in.

The band was well into the warm-up number when a spotlight picked up Al Hirt at the rear of the club, walking slowly in the aisle, which sloped down to the bandstand, playing along with the band as he came. It was a dramatic touch that I never failed to enjoy.

Toward the end of the show, Al graciously introduced me, noting that I was chaplain of Pete Fountain's Walking Club. He spoke favorably of the invocation that I had delivered and mentioned the price tag on it.

"Come on up here, Father, and play a couple of numbers with us."

I hurried up to the bandstand. The memory of the thrill of that moment will remain with me all my days. As I returned to my seat he thanked me for playing and added:

"You can sit in with my band anytime you want."

I took him at his word and often did so in the years that followed. Our invariable routine proved to be "Just a Closer Walk" followed by "Mood Indigo" as an encore. Some years later, when Al Hirt closed the doors of his club for good, that happy ritual went out of my life.

During my walk on Mardi Gras Day with Pete Fountain's Walking Club around 1986 or '87, we stopped briefly on the corner of St. Louis and Bourbon Street. There I read on the façade of the building that was once Al Hirt's Club: *Ripley's Believe It Or Not Museum*. A twinge of sadness touched my heart. Then we struck up the band and moved away.

C H A P T E R   1 6

Fundamentalists and Green Frogs

Y EAR AFTER YEAR, THE ZEALOUS YOUNG
fundamentalists come to the Mardi Gras in New Orleans. They do not come to participate, but to protest.

Year after year, we Half-Fast walkers encounter them,
usually on Bourbon Street. They come armed with bibles
and banners. Their banners have such captions as "Jesus
Saves" (to which I agree wholeheartedly) or "Repent"
(which I wholly endorse).

There are printed reminders that damnation awaits the
unrepentant sinner. There is the omnipresent "John 3:16."
(Those who watch sports on TV can attest that this text
has attended more athletic contests than the most ardent
of sports enthusiasts.)

One of our members once paused long enough to surprise the young fundamentalists by quoting John 3:16 in
full:

"God so loved the world that he gave his only Son so
that everyone who believes in him may not be lost but

they may have eternal life."

My fellow walker believes this. I believe this. Most of our members are Christian who also believe this.

My quarrel is not with the mainstream theology of the banner-bearers. What disturbs me is the mentality I perceive behind their presence and gesture, and the image of God that it projects.

I have participated in the New Orleans Mardi Gras, as spectator and walker, close to forty times. For the past twenty-three years I have walked with Pete Fountain's Half-Fasters. I have been on my feet and in the very thick of it every one of those years for about six hours, over a route of several miles and through hundreds of thousands of revellers.

I admit that I have seen my share of ugliness and evil, ranging from bad taste to downright immorality. But on a scale of one to ten, I would estimate that kind of behavior to be a fraction of one. I do not have a sense of being a part of one titanic outdoor orgy of sin when I walk on Mardi Gras Day. I feel rather that I am part of and contributing to a gigantic, joyous outdoor party, truly the "Greatest Free Show on Earth." Now, admittedly, it has its abuses, but it does brighten for a day the dullness of the lives of countless thousands of good people.

When I first saw the young banner-bearing fundamentalists, my immediate reaction was resentment, but I have long since put that response behind me. It is not a rational response. It is not a Christian response. I have, on reflection, come rather to admire them for their sincerity, goodwill and courage. I know they must have to take some verbal abuse – but never, to my knowledge, from a member of our Walking Club. I praise them for their willingness to expose themselves to the inevitability of abuse.

I respect them as persons but cannot accept their implied image of God and their view of what does or does not constitute Christian behavior.

In my most recent Mardi Gras walk with Pete Fountain I looked for the young fundamentalists, but they were not out on Bourbon Street nor Royal Street nor any of the side streets as we meandered through the French Quarter. I missed them. What I did see, however, to my utter disgust and dismay, was a walking, blasphemous parody of these good young people. It was on Bourbon Street, and I am happy they were not there to see it.

We turned off Canal Street onto Bourbon and stopped, as we do every year, in the middle of the 200 block and filed into Carlo Montalbano's fine restaurant to be the guests of that generous and genial gentleman. We ate, drank and cooled our heels at this welcome oasis. After we had spilled back onto Bourbon Street and were making our way deeper into the Quarter, I spotted them: The Green Frogs.

They were a group of a half-dozen or so young men and women, dressed as green frogs. Like my fundamentalist friends, whom they were satirizing, they were carrying banners. One read: "Green Frog Saves." Another, "Green Frog Croaked For Your Sins."

I was appalled and deeply pained at this display of mindless mockery. To disagree with the convictions of a person – be he Jew, Muslim, Hindu, Christian, agnostic or atheist – is one thing; to *mock* a person's beliefs is quite another. It is intolerable because it targets not the beliefs but the person of the believer.

St. Paul wept because there were, from the beginning, "enemies of the Crucified Christ." He referred to the Cross of Christ as a "stumbling block" to Jews and an "absurdity" to Gentiles. That some experience the Cross of Christ as a stumbling block or honestly view it as an absurdity is understandable, and I respect them. But I find it to be vicious when one chooses to *mock* my belief in the Cross of Christ and all that it stands for and has meant to me and hundreds of millions of Christians down through the centuries.

Perhaps those young people were merely thoughtless and were only trying to be funny. I hope so. And I hope and pray that one day they will come to realize that their demonstration was, objectively, unjust and unkind.

And I even dare to hope and pray that some day they will come to share the belief that he who said from the Cross, "Father forgive them, for they know not what they do," was born, lived and died for all, even the Green Frogs of Mardi Gras 1988.

CHAPTER 17

Preach?
I just did!

ONCE I HAD THE UNEXPECTED PRIVILEGE of sitting in with the late, great Zoot Sims. Zoot was a renowned tenor saxophone player, who, when I met him in New Orleans during a run at the Hyatt-Regency Hotel, was also playing a lot of first-rate soprano sax.

Zoot did not live to see sixty. Not long before he died, he was honored by his peers, a large number of prominent musicians, with a timely surprise birthday party at sea on an all-star jazz cruise.

Although I brought my clarinet with me to the Hyatt (just in case) I really did not expect to be invited to sit in. Even before I sat down, however, I felt I had a chance, because I noticed that Zoot was using a local drummer, my good friend Freddie Kohlman. Freddie knows I love to play, and I knew he would put in a good word for me. Musicians vary greatly in their willingness to let players, known or unknown, sit in with their bands.

Zoot proved to be gracious, for after one set Freddie

came to my table to chat and to inform me that Zoot was going to call me up. As the second set got underway, I assembled my clarinet, moistened my reed and was at the ready.

When I had finished playing "Just A Closer Walk," I got a taste of Zoot's wry humor. He looked up from his chair – Zoot sat while he played – and said:

"That's nice. Do you know anything else?"

I laughed.

"A couple more tunes. Let's do 'Willow, Weep For Me.'"

I remember Zoot doing some marvelous choruses on "Willow" that night. Before I left the bandstand he said:

"I like some of the things you did on that number." Then he remarked that he was "always learning," and I thought: *Learning? From me?*

The only time I ever conversed with Zoot Sims was that evening at the Hyatt, but I came away feeling that I knew the man. I felt I had met a gracious gentleman and a true artist with poise and grace, a master of his instruments.

What I remember most vividly about that pleasant evening is a remark that came out of the audience, near the bandstand, when we had finished playing "Closer Walk."

"You going to preach us a sermon now, Reverend?" someone asked.

In a sudden flash of inspiration, I fired back:

"I just did."

Priests and other ministers of the Gospel preach sermons with words, but there are other ways. Actions preach more eloquently than words. Being present and being what you are called to be constitute an ongoing sermon that varies, to be sure, in effectiveness.

Possibly my inspiration to say "I just did" rose from the unconscious memory of a well-worn story told in religious circles. It is the story of an elderly monk who asked a young monk to accompany him to town, where he was going to preach a sermon. They walked through the streets of the town, smiling and greeting the townsfolk and then returned to the monastery.

"You didn't preach the sermon," said the young monk.

"Yes, we did," the elderly monk responded.

I firmly believe that priestly presence in any milieu can have sacramental value. In that sense I do not think a priest is ever off duty. And in the context of ministerial presence, opportunities will come for direct ministry. I am always ready and willing to seize them. Two such opportunities, among many, stand out. I cherish them. One concerned Lou Sino.

It was always exciting to be present when my good friend Lou Sino was performing. He was a remarkable trombonist, a vigorous jazz vocalist, who jumped and quivered as he sang. A supreme showman, his trademark was a pyrotechnic rendition of "Tiger Rag." I had heard of Lou during his years with Louie Prima's band. I was delighted to learn that Lou had quit the road and decided to come home. I discovered him at a little club in New Orleans called The Bistro, on Tulane Avenue, just a few blocks from Jesuit High, where I was teaching at that time. I walked over there one evening to hear him and, as ever, hoping to sit in.

Lou lived up to his advanced billing. I was enthralled. I discovered, too, that night a plus in the person of Rene Netto, one of the very best reed men in New Orleans. He excels on tenor sax, and is very capable on clarinet and flute.

Rene, working with Lou in those days, later formed his own band. Sadly, the last time I saw Rene he was working at a day job at Schubert's Marine Sales and Service in New Orleans' West End. Over lunch I tried to help him work his way through a vexing personal problem. All he was doing musically at that time was taking occasional "spot jobs." It is disconcerting how many talented musicians have to curtail or even discontinue their musical activities and take a day job to support themselves and their families.

Before that evening at The Bistro was over, I was rejoicing that I had discovered a musical bonanza right in my own back yard.

Someone in the band knew me and introduced me to Lou Sino between sets. He obligingly let me sit in that evening and many evenings thereafter both at The Bistro and in half a dozen other clubs in the New Orleans area.

My fondest memories of Lou and his band came a few years later, in the early '70s, when he was alternating nightly with the The Ronnie Kole Trio at the Royal Sonesta Hotel in the French Quarter. The tourist trade was brisk in those prosperous days. Economy Hall, located in the basement of the Royal Sonesta, was often packed. But, like so many other clubs in the Quarter featuring the kind of music I love, it went the way of Al Hirt's club.

It was at Economy Hall, between sets, that a door opened on an opportunity for priestly ministry that brought some consolation into the married life of Lou and Pat Sino. Lou made his request casually.

"Father, I've got to talk to you about something when we finish up tonight."

"Sure, Lou. Be glad to," I said.

It was after hours, about 1 a.m., when we sat down to talk.

"My wife and I are Catholics, and we want to get back to the practice of our religion," he began.

It was a familiar story: two young people, in love, impatient, anxious to get married, by-passing the requirements and conditions of the Church, short-cutting their way to the office of the Justice of the Peace.

"We've been wanting to get our marriage blessed in the Church and get back to practicing our religion. We just haven't got around to it yet," he explained.

"You say you are both Catholics?"

"Yes."

"Had either of you been married before?" (*The* question.)

"No."

I know I breathed a sigh of relief.

"No problem then," I said. "I can get this fixed up for you in no time. What's your parish church?"

He did not know.

"I haven't been going to church much, but I want to get back to it."

Within a week the paperwork was done and arrangements were made. On a Saturday afternoon five persons stood in front of rows of empty pews, before the altar of St. Cletus Church in Gretna. The lifetime commitment that Lou and Pat had made years before was supplemented by the long-missing, beautiful ceremony in the Church. According to the teaching of the Church, this ceremony conveys the relayed blessing and grace of Jesus Christ.

We were only five. I officiated. The pastor and a friend of Pat's were the witnesses. Pat cried. Then we all went into the rectory, signed some papers, and had a celebratory drink. That night, I was at Economy Hall, and Lou – who had few inhibitions – thanked me publicly.

"Father married Pat and me this afternoon. A honeymoon with five kids along is going to be hell!" Lou announced.

Lou re-discovered his Catholic faith and later the Bible. In his last years he was reading and reflecting on the Scripture – which led to our between-sets discussions on the occasions that I was able to come to hear and play with his band before his untimely death.

May this talented entertainer, who was possessed of such fiery energy, rest in peace.

CHAPTER 18

A Weekend Miracle

ANOTHER DOOR OF OPPORTUNITY FOR ministry and healing was opened to me by Ronnie Dupont, a musician in Al Hirt's band.

Not long after we met, Ronnie began to confide in me, usually before he went on the bandstand, sometimes after hours. He was burdened with emotional problems, marital problems and, typically, with the accompanying symptom of immoderate drinking.

One evening, before going on at Al Hirt's club, he came to my table and said he needed to talk to me in private. We found a quiet corner.

He was deeply depressed. He described a distressing and emotion-packed conflict that had recently occurred between him and his wife. He then extended his left hand, revealing a nasty cut.

"I can play, but it's not easy," he said. "I've got to do something about this. I've got to get my life straightened out. This could have ended my career."

As always in these brief encounters, I experienced frustration in the face of so much pain and so little time to reach out and try to heal. To be sure, listening with sympathy is important therapy, a practice that has been called "uh-huh therapy." But one always wants to do more.

"Come see me when we have more time. Let's make an appointment…" My invariable conclusion would be: "What you need is to come out to our place and make a retreat. You have to take a weekend off and come out to our place and think and pray and consult and sort things out and get your life together."

It seemed that nothing would ever come of my exhortations. Then one blessed day I got a phone call and the door of opportunity swung wide open. The voice was urgent, almost desperate.

"Father, I've got to come see you. I've got to talk to you."

"Where are you calling from?" I asked.

"I'm in New Orleans. At home, in Harvey."

"I'm a hundred and fifty miles away from where you are," I told him.

At that time I was stationed at Our Lady of the Oaks Retreat House in Grand Coteau.

"I don't care. How do I get there?"

"When are you coming?"

"Anytime. You name it."

"How about tomorrow morning?"

"I'll be there. How do I get there?"

"Take I-10 to Lafayette. Take the Highway 167 exit north. It's about ten miles to the Grand Coteau exit. You'll pass Evangeline Downs… Look," I continued, "tomorrow is Thursday. I'm giving a retreat that begins tomorrow night. Let me sign you up to make this retreat. We have room. It ends at midday on Sunday. You working this weekend?"

"No. But I don't want to make a retreat. No, no. I've

just got to talk to you."

"Well, think about it. Come on. I'm free all morning. I'll be on the lookout for you."

On arrival he told me he decided to stay and make the retreat. It was a couple of years later when I learned what went into his decision to make the retreat in addition to the grace of God, which was surely at work. I learned it from a letter he sent from Singapore, where he had a six-month engagement playing in a jazz quartet at the Westin Stamford Hotel. He wrote:

"You know, before I got into my car to go to your retreat house I had to stop at Betty Assunto's house to drink a bunch of vodka to get the nerve to go." (Betty, a singing star of the original Dukes of Dixieland, is the widow of that famed band's trombonist, Freddie Assunto.)

I know of no short-range investment of time that can reap such enormous and far-reaching spiritual dividends as a three-day retreat, well-made. I have seen this moral miracle wrought on numerous weekends. It happens in an atmosphere of silence. Silence on a retreat is a must. Into that all-pervading silence comes a sense of the nearness of God. There are talks to attend. There are priests available for private conferences. There is a well-stocked library. But all these are nothing more than catalysts, more or less dispensable.

The essential happening is that you have come face-to-face with your God, with Jesus Christ. You have come face-to-face with your naked self. And all this is happening in the atmosphere of peaceful silence, under the rays of the eternal truths of the Christian faith. In the light of all this, you look at your life, past, present and future. Spiritually you ask: *Where have I been? Where am I? Where am I headed? Where ought I to be headed?* You think. You pray. You make resolutions.

For my musician friend Ronnie, that weekend at Our Lady of the Oaks was a death and a resurrection. In the language of St. Paul, the old self died and a new self rose. The grim Good Friday of his arrival was, after the three-day descent into the silent depths of retreat, followed by a resurrection. The glow of Easter was in his face when he left Grand Coteau that Sunday afternoon.

Years later, I read in his letter from Singapore:

"I tell you, Father, if I hadn't gone to retreat when I did I wouldn't be here right now. I was drinking too much and was deeply depressed, but that all changed from the time I went, thanks to the Lord's help and yours. I have beat the depression and don't drink anymore. Feels great to be alive again."

Blessed be jazz!

CHAPTER 19

'Just a Closer Walk'

EVEN BEFORE I REACHED MY TEENS I HAD become an ardent baseball fan. I became aware of organized baseball in the form of my hometown's semi-pro team, the Helena Seaporters, who played twice a week.

Many of these team members were college football players on summer vacation, from Mississippi State, Ole Miss, Alabama and other, mostly Southern, colleges and universities. Alabama's Don Hutson, All-American, and later All-Pro for the Green Bay Packers, played left field one summer for the Seaporters.

Later Helena joined the Class C Cotton States League, and so my two-mile hikes to the ball park in the summer heat became more frequent. Our bitter rival was the nearby Clarksdale, Miss., team. Their ace pitcher was a lean lefthander whose name was "Red" Mackey.

The road through life takes some strange twists and turns, for more than forty years later, in Opelousas, La., I sat one evening with Red Mackey's daughter, Jeanette, reviewing a yellowed newspaper clipping, the account of a game that Red Mackey pitched against the Helena Seaporters.

Jeanette and her husband, Dr. George Bourgeois, are dear friends of mine. I met them shortly before they married. She was a widow with one child; he was a widower with four. I have spent many an enjoyable evening with them and their children, mostly with "hers" (Kristin) and "theirs" (Jason and Rachal).

Kristin is a tiny package of dynamite on the basketball court. Jason is slender, handsome and athletic and may well be on the pro golf tour some day. Rachal, poised beyond her years and quite attractive, at age thirteen single-handedly recruited her mother's friends and organized them into a surprise birthday party for her mother. Rachal may well become the first woman president of the United States.

One evening while visiting the Bourgeoises, I learned that Jeanette was Red Mackey's daughter. She brought out her scrapbook, where I read the clipping about her dad's pitching against my old team. And the ghosts of a long-dead past came floating up into my conscious memory.

Among the joys of socializing with the Bourgeoises, was getting to know "Maman," Jeanette's maternal grandmother. Maman was well into her eighties when I met her and ninety-four when she finally decided to let go and return to her Maker. Even in the last year of her life, before those final, pain-wracked, dying weeks, I remember her sitting erect, her snow-white hair combed back neatly, a smile or a near-smile always on her face and a twinkle in her eye. She was determined, fiercely independent. At age sixty, shortly after her husband's death, she learned how to drive an automobile. In her forties, she became co-owner and eventually sole owner of a women's apparel shop, *La Petite Shoppe*, and ran it successfully for forty-seven years. At age ninety, she decided to retire.

It was a privilege for me to play, at Jeanette's request, "Just a Closer Walk" at Maman's funeral. Fr. Mike Arnaud, who delivered the eulogy, expertly summed up her personality when he suggested that, now in heaven, she was probably trying to "sell Jesus some clothes for His mother."

Playing "Just A Closer Walk" on the clarinet at funerals has become a kind of sub-avocation for me. I have done so a number of times and have been asked to do so by many friends and acquaintances, some of whom will surely outlive me. "Closer Walk" at a funeral is, in this part of the South, like motherhood, the American flag and apple pie.

Claiborne Perrilliat Sr., known to his family as "Papa" (accent on the last syllable), did not make an explicit request that I play "Closer Walk" or, for that matter, any other selection at his funeral, but the fact that I did would have surely met with his full approval. Papa had let it be known that he wanted no manifestations of sorrow at his wake or funeral.

"You can bring in a jazz band at my funeral," he had said.

His son, Claiborne Jr., took him at his word and, consequently, the day before the funeral, phoned me and asked if I could get some jazz musicians together to play at the funeral. I knew this would be next to impossible on short notice. I suggested that I do my version of "Closer Walk" without accompaniment during the Communion of the Mass. He agreed and added that Papa would have endorsed the concept.

For a weekday afternoon, the crowd in Holy Name of Jesus Church on St. Charles Avenue in New Orleans was surprisingly large. The eulogist was Fr. Ed Donahue, SJ, who was director of Manresa Retreat House when Papa Perrilliat began making retreats there. Papa logged twenty-nine retreats in all. I can recall being at Manresa when he attended his last retreat, getting about in a wheelchair, failing, but cheerful and courageous to the end.

Fr. Donahue told his story well and elicited more smiles than tears as he did so. Papa would have liked that, too.

It was with a full heart and a deep sense of joy that I stood at the mic in the sanctuary during Communion to express with my clarinet, bare and unaccompanied, what was in my heart that afternoon. I would not have traded that moment for one in Carnegie Hall.

The funeral of Claiborne Perrilliat Sr. took place in 1980. I did not know that his friend "Buddy" Frazer was in the congregation that afternoon. In fact, I did not even know Buddy Frazer existed until I read, seven years later, on the obituary page of the New Orleans *Times-Picayune*, the impressive account of his life, character and achievements. He was in his mid-fifties when he died of cancer. Buddy was the manager of the New Orleans public TV station and an active and successful civic figure.

To my surprise, the following day I received a phone call from the music director of the St. Charles Avenue Presbyterian Church, the church Buddy Frazer attended. I was informed by the caller that in his final illness Buddy had requested that I play "Just A Closer Walk" at his funeral. Puzzled and delighted, I accepted the invitation. Only later did I learn the solution to the puzzle.

"I'll be glad to," I said to the music director. "When is the funeral?"

"Tomorrow. At 11 a.m."

"I'd like to have an accompanist if possible."

"I play organ, piano and guitar," he said.

"Let's go with piano. Can I come over and run through it with you? I play it in *F*."

We agreed on a time.

It was a small step for ecumenism and, all in all, a moving experience for me, a Roman Catholic priest in a Presbyterian church, playing a gospel song neither Catholic nor Presbyterian. In his eulogy, the pastor added a note of ecumenism by reading a psalm from the Jerusalem Bible (a Roman Catholic translation) and quoting a well-known Catholic spiritual writer, Fr. Henri Nouwen. Fr. Nouwen's image of entering Heaven included stepping out of an airplane to be greeted by Jesus with the words, "Welcome home, Henri. Let me look at your slides." The eulogy was warm and touchingly personal.

I left the church in a glow of gratitude to God for the gift of music and its magnetic power to draw unrelated people together. Blessed be jazz!

Estelle Mayer was another person whom I had never met, but who made a request that I play "Closer Walk" at her funeral. Nor was she a member of the Catholic Church. Estelle was a member of Epiphany Episcopal Church in Opelousas, La., a widow, a retired school teacher. After she was informed that she had terminal cancer, she calmly set about planning her funeral to the last detail.

It happened that I was included in those plans, because she had heard and thought well of my album, "A Closer Walk With Three." The album was a gift to her from my friend Dr. George Bourgeois, who attended her in her final illness. During one of his visits to her home, she had made the request. He promised to relay the message to me, and he did so on one of my visits to his home.

"Of course," I assured him.

"I'll tell her the next time I visit her."

"I'd like to tell her myself. Let's go to her home some day and let me reassure her that I will play at her funeral."

I regret that it took me so long to get around to paying Estelle that first visit. "Get around to it," is a sorry mask we put on the face of sloth. I regret it because I managed only two visits before her death. I regret, too, that I had not met her long before, for Estelle Mayer was one charming person, full of a *joie de vivre* that belied the cancer within her. The disease was smothering her life but could not smother her spirit.

When George asked her if he could bring me over on that eventful Sunday afternoon, she replied that she would be honored. When I asked her permission to include her story in my book, she said she would be honored. But before that first visit was over, I knew who the real honoree was.

She sat up with dignity in her chair, detailing her funeral arrangements with the casualness of one planning a party. Indeed, there were some aspects of a party about her funeral. Witness her directive to serve refreshments to all who attended, as soon as the funeral services were completed. And a consummate touch of class: for her relatives and the chosen few who attended her burial, a round of drinks in the lounge of the Steamboat Warehouse, a quaint restaurant perched above Bayou Courtableau in Washington, La. By her request, this bayou received her ashes on a lovely, sun-drenched Friday afternoon.

In our first conversation, she revealed that she had heard me play a number of times in Opelousas, fifteen or so years earlier, at Toby's Little Lodge with Rev. Lionel Reason. (This is a story that I will try to do justice to in another chapter.) I spent many an enjoyable evening there in the seventies. It was a bittersweet moment for me when she told me she had been in the audience during some of those evenings. I felt a surge of joy that my playing had pleased her, but a pang of regret that I had only now come to know it.

Her thin body appeared frail and weak, but her mind was still razor-sharp. I noticed that she had been working a *New York Times* crossword puzzle. I commented that I was a former high school English teacher and had a certain addiction to crossword puzzles.

"*The New York Times* puzzles are the best," she said. "I'll have copies made for you of the ones I have."

My second (and final) visit to her was very touching. Again, it was a Sunday afternoon. By then she was confined to her bed. Dr. Bourgeois was with me. She observed, but in a matter of fact way, not in the least complaining, that her eyesight was fading and that she had no strength left. It was clear, even to my layman's eye, that she was at the beginning of the end. I knew she would not live out the week.

She smiled at me.

"Here are your puzzles," she said.

They were lying on the bed beside her. She handed them to me.

"You remembered!" I exclaimed.

"Oh, yes."

On Wednesday Estelle's brother phoned to say she had died Tuesday evening. The funeral service was to be Friday morning; the burial, Friday afternoon.

"I'll be there," I promised.

The crowd that crammed the hall at Lafond-Ardoin Funeral Home attested to the love and esteem so many in the Opelousas community had for Estelle Mayer. We followed, with but one exception, the directives she had left, set down in her own hand, signed and dated Dec. 22, 1987.

> *To my family –*
> *Instructions for a brief service for me*
> *Music for processional is to be "Just A Closer Walk With Thee" – Fr. Coco*
> *Have a brief prayer by the priest*
> *Then "The Lord's Prayer" by soloist*
> *Next a prayer by Coy Pavy (a friend)*
> *And then I wish for all present to join in singing "America The Beautiful"*
> *Music for the recessional shall be "How Great Thou Art" by Fr. Coco*
> *The ashes are then to be taken to Washington, Louisiana, and sprinkled in Bayou Courtableau*
>   *– Estelle B. Mayer*

That simple burial service on the shores of Bayou Courtableau is forever stamped in my memory. After I had read some brief prayers, a tall, handsome young man (her nephew, Tom Brès) walked solemnly down the unpainted wooden steps leading from the landing to the water's edge, carrying an opaque rectangular black box in which one could dimly discern a bag. It was no bigger than an average-sized lady's purse, containing all that was left of Estelle Mayer on earth.

She had requested that the bag containing her ashes be paper (the only directive that her family could not bring themselves to follow), for to the end Estelle was concerned about the environment and thought that paper would least offend the environment.

Tom opened the box carefully and out slid the bag into the water. He gave it a gentle push, and it floated away on the slow current of the tan water, and the bubbling revealed that Estelle's ashes were filtering down and mingling with the Louisiana she loved.

Estelle Brès Mayer went "gently into that dark night." And I have no doubt that her bright spirit is lighting up some corner of God's Heaven.

The Beauty of Friendship

*B*Y AND LARGE, MY MANY EXCURSIONS INTO the world of jazz music have put me in contact with hundreds of good and agreeable people. Were it not for my appearances, wearing my Roman collar, on the bandstand, however, I suspect I would have come and gone unnoticed by them.

But once I have been on the bandstand and made my contribution to the kind of music they came to hear, the lines of communication open up instantly and conversation with people I have never seen before easily follows. I expect this and I welcome it.

I count three categories of positive encounters on these occasions. I think of **Category 1** as hello-and-goodbye encounters. People come briefly into my life, we talk, and they go out of it forever.

Playing with a jazz group at a brunch once on the patio of The Court of Two Sisters, I met the vivacious Mary Martin of *South Pacific* and *Peter Pan* fame. She was altogether charming.

"I'm sorry," I said, as I introduced myself to her. "I didn't recognize you at first."

"Why should you?" she asked and smiled and immediately stepped out of the spotlight to talk about her son.

"Do you watch *Dallas*? J.R. is my son, you know."

At Al Hirt's club I met the movie great Pat O'Brien, whom Al brought on stage to take a bow and tell an Irish joke. When he learned I was a Jesuit he was quick to inform me that he was a "Jesuit boy," having attended Marquette University in Milwaukee.

In Pete Fountain's club, I once heard screen actor Robert Mitchum call out in a booming voice: "Play 'Memphis Blues,' Pete." (Mitchum is from Tennessee.)

I had the pleasure of meeting him in Pete's den backstage after the show. He had recently returned from Vietnam, where he had spent part of his vacation. Somehow he had managed to get permission to visit the battlefield, where he drank martinis, he told us, with an officer whose wife was smuggling them in through the mail in shave lotion or mouthwash containers. When he returned to the States, Mitchum thoughtfully phoned her to say, "Thanks for the martinis."

Also in Category 1 are those good folk who express wistful thoughts.

"I wish my daughter could meet you. She's stopped going to Mass;" or "My son could relate to a priest like you. He doesn't practice his religion anymore;" or "If I had met a priest like you I would never have left the Church."

The implied premise is clearly that a priest who will get up and swing with professional jazz musicians must be an "all-right guy." The logic may be faulty, but the connections are made frequently, nevertheless.

Among my favorites in Category 1 are not the celebrities or the wistful ones, but the alumnae and alumni of Jesuit high schools, colleges and universities. As soon as they learn that "The Father with the horn" is a Jesuit priest, they invariably reveal their identity as grads of Jesuit schools. They feel right at home with a "Jebbie," and I must say it is mutual.

There are in the United States forty-six Jesuit high schools and twenty-eight colleges and universities. The alumnae and alumni of these institutions make up one huge, informal fraternity-sorority. The number of living graduates of Jesuit colleges and universities is more than one million; of Jesuit high schools, it is about 250,000.

I frequently hear questions and comments like this:

"Do you happen to know Fr. So-and-so at Santa Clara? Did my undergraduate studies there."

"Fr. X at Fordham. Do you know him? Great teacher. Had him for philosophy."

"Do you ever get up to the Baltimore area? I graduated from Loyola. Fr. Sellinger…a great guy."

"So you're a 'Jebbie'? Well, they brainwashed me too!"

"I figured you were either an Episcopalian priest or a Jesuit." This from a member of the staff of St. Louis University.

The fellowship that always seems to come when the Jesuit connection is realized is a heart-warming experience for me. And it happens over and over again.

Category 2 is comprised of those who came into my life and stayed, not as intimate friends, for distance and opportunity precluded so deep a relationship, but with whom I have been able to maintain a friendly association by occasional correspondence and even, on rare occasions, a visit. These are people with whom, given the opportunity of consistent presence and communication, I am sure I would reach the intimacy of true friendship – which I think of as the ultimate, Category 3.

In Category 2 I count a couple from New Jersey who came to New Orleans to attend a Sugar Bowl football

game. They were Pitt Panther fans. I met them at the New
Orleans Hilton, the temporary headquarters of the Pitt
team. We got acquainted in the downstairs area known as
Café Bromeliad, where I happened to be sitting in with
Sandy Cash's musical group. The New Jersey couple enjoyed my playing with the band and expressed an interest
in my album. At their request, I mailed them one. We have
kept in touch through the mail. At Christmastime I will receive a card with a personal note and a check, which they
include as a Christmas gift.

I have met a considerable number of people in this category, who I am sure would expect me to phone them and,
if possible, drop in on them if I happened to be in their
vicinity.

I have come to believe that the full bloom of friendship comes only after one has come to know a person well
– which requires a certain frequency of presence and long,
ongoing, open communication. We often use the word
"friend" too loosely and casually, for want of a satisfactory distinguishing term. "Acquaintance" works sometimes,
but often does not say enough. I would certainly consider
the people in my Category 2 much more than mere acquaintances.

People in Category 2 sometimes move into **Category 3**.
One example of such a transition is my friendship with the
Espositos.

Two couples, the Espositos and the Butters, from Elmira,
N.Y., were on a vacation tour of the Cajun country and
were dining at Lafayette's superb Riverside Inn. I was at a
nearby table introducing two fellow Jesuits from the Mary-
land Province to the delights of Cajun cuisine. The subject
of jazz music came up, and I expressed regret that my two
Jesuit brothers had to leave town immediately after dinner,
as I had wanted to take them to the lounge of Toby's Oak
Grove and play for them at the weekly Wednesday night
jazz jam session. Carmen Esposito overheard the reference

to jazz and came to our table to introduce himself and make inquiries. He quickly informed me that he had attended two Jesuit universities, John Carroll in Cleveland, Ohio, and University of Detroit. A "double whammy," he called it.

"Pardon me, Father, but did I hear you say that you are a Jesuit and that you play jazz? Where can we find jazz around here?"

"At Toby's, in the lounge," I answered. "How long are you going to be in town?"

"A couple more days. I know where Toby's is," he said. "We passed it. It's not too far from our motel."

"Tell you what…I have to get these two Jesuits to their car. They have to get on the road. They have to catch a plane out of New Orleans early tomorrow morning. Suppose I meet you at Toby's, say, about 8 or 8:30? I'll play a few tunes for you."

It proved to be an enjoyable evening for them and for me. We were very soon quite at ease with one another. Since that evening we have kept in touch.

That autumn both couples had occasion to come to the Boston area. I was on a six-months sabbatical in Cambridge, Mass., at the Weston Jesuit School of Theology. They took the time and trouble to visit with me. We spent a Sunday afternoon together, which included dinner in one of my favorite places in the USA – the Italian section of North End Boston. A couple of years later, having kept in touch with the Espositos by phone and letter, I had a happy reunion with them in Dallas. Thus, does a Category 2 friendship evolve into a Category 3.

Among the persons who have entered my life, to whom the sacred word "friend" applies in all its fullness, are Larry and Kathlyn Hurst of Lafayette, Louisiana. It was jazz that brought us together in the early 1970s. We have remained the closest of friends.

The Royal Sonesta Hotel's Economy Hall was quite

crowded that evening in 1971, even though it was early in the week. I sat in with Lou Sino's band and remember playing as my final number "What Is This Thing Called Love?" I had not noticed the lone lady seated near the bandstand.

I returned to my table and to my unfinished drink. I was alone. Lou Sino was concluding his set when my waitress came to my table and set a drink in front of me.

"The lady over there near the bandstand asked me to bring you a drink," the waitress said, tilting her head in the general direction of my benefactress.

I looked and saw a beautiful face turned my way, smiling and nodding. She sat very erect, with a queenly bearing.

After Lou had finished the set and while The Ronnie Kole Trio settled in to begin theirs, I made my way to the lady's table.

"Thank you for the drink," I said.

With a nod, she acknowledged my expression of gratitude but quickly brushed it aside.

"I'm surprised to see a priest playing jazz in a night club on Bourbon Street," she said. "I've never seen anything like that before."

"Well, this is New Orleans," I explained. "Where else but in New Orleans? Are you a tourist or local?"

"I don't live here, but I'm not exactly a tourist. I live in Lafayette, La. I come to New Orleans often, maybe once a month."

I learned that she and her husband owned and operated a restaurant in Lafayette, Poor Boy's Riverside Inn. Her husband's choice of a break was a weekly day of fishing in the Atchafalaya Basin; hers was the periodic trip to New Orleans early in the week. Since restaurateurs and retreat directors are about their business on weekends, our mid-week chance encounter wasn't particularly surprising. I have always said that my "weekend" begins on Sunday evening. Many a Monday, Tuesday or Wednesday would find me at Economy Hall, basking in the music of Ronnie Kole, Lou Sino and René Netto.

Kathlyn Hurst was and is an ardent Ronnie Kole fan, as am I, and had happily discovered saxophonist René Netto, starring in Lou Sino's great group, as had I. And she was simply in love with New Orleans – its food, its atmosphere, its music and the Royal Sonesta and Economy Hall.

"So, you're from Lafayette. I suppose you know where Grand Coteau is then. I did my first four years of Jesuit training there, at St. Charles College, '38 to '42. And I was stationed there one year as a young priest."

"I guess I do know where Grand Coteau is! I went to school at the Academy there for eight years. I started in the fifth grade."

We were on common ground.

There are four Catholic institutions in the little township of Grand Coteau, fifteen miles or so north of Lafayette, the oldest being the prestigious Academy of the Sacred Heart, a girls' school, founded in 1821. The other three are Jesuit institutions: St. Charles Borromeo Parish Church, Our Lady of the Oaks Retreat House, and St. Charles College, which serves now as both a spirituality center and Jesuit Novitiate.

On a couple of occasions after our first encounter in 1971 I ran into Kathlyn, and it was on an evening in June of that year that I informed her that I had just received from my superior the shock of my life. After seventeen years I was being transferred out of the New Orleans area.

"Where will you be going?"

"To Grand Coteau. Our Lady of the Oaks Retreat House."

"Oh, good! Then you can meet my husband and my children. And you can come to our restaurant and…"

I interrupted.

"Good? It's a disaster!"

I was in only my first year of retreat work at Manresa Retreat House after sixteen years of teaching high school in New Orleans and was enjoying one of the happiest years of my Jesuit life. I was dismayed at the prospect of leaving.

So, in mid-August I moved to Grand Coteau. Although it is less than 150 miles west of New Orleans, one would have thought I was moving to *ultima Thule*. I went willingly but with a heavy heart, a head full of fond memories, and a determination to make the best of it.

The first couple of weeks were hectic, and the quieter moments were laced with depression. Near the end of the month I decided to drive to the Riverside Inn in Lafayette to accept Kathlyn's luncheon invitation, which she had tendered a few months earlier. When I arrived at the entrance of the restaurant, I saw a sign taped to the door: "CLOSED. ON VACATION." I settled for a forlorn lunch for one at Don's Seafood, thinking I would have to wait a week or so to renew our acquaintance and to meet Kathlyn's husband, Larry.

It turned out, however, that I was to see Kathlyn and meet Larry sooner than I had expected. This was because of a promise I had made to my sister, Rita, who is a member of a religious community, the Sisters of Charity of Nazareth (Kentucky).

I had promised Rita that I would help her experience the sights and sounds of New Orleans on her summer vacation, never anticipating that I would be transferred out of the New Orleans area. This promise afforded me a legitimate opening to return to my old haunts some two weeks after I had arrived in Grand Coteau. At the head of the list of our agenda was a trip to Economy Hall.

As my sister and I were making our way to our table at Economy Hall, whom did we encounter but Kathlyn Hurst with her husband in tow! Somehow she had seduced him, this lover of fishing in the Atchafalaya Basin, into coming with her to spend a few days of their vacation in New Orleans. Kathlyn introduced us to Larry. I introduced my sister to Kathlyn. We were off to a relaxed and happy evening.

A few days later, my sister accompanied me as I returned to Grand Coteau and reality.

Eventually, I had my lunch at Riverside Inn, the first of many meals at one of Lafayette's oldest and finest restaurants, ably run today by Elaine and Richard, daughter and son of Larry and Kathlyn Hurst. Larry is out now, breathing God's air, where he loves to be, farming crawfish. Kathlyn, a great chef, is working for her son and daughter.

On a memorable Sunday afternoon I met the rest of the Hurst family: Kathlyn's mother, Eugenia Landry, widow of the founder of Riverside Inn, and the four children, then quite young – Patti, Elaine, Debbi and Richard.

Sunday afternoons and evenings with the Hursts became an important part of my week. I began to share the joys and sorrows, the tragedies and the triumphs of a family that will be ever dear to me.

In those first weeks of transition, I would have been willing to walk back to Manresa dragging my luggage, had I been permitted to return. But within a few months I found peace of mind and heart in Grand Coteau. I gradually fell in love with Our Lady of the Oaks and the good people who came to our retreats. Within my own little Jesuit family I found the companionship, encouragement and support that went a long way toward bringing that peace.

We were three priests at Our Lady of the Oaks. The other two were Frs. Dan Partridge, the director, and Ed Goss. Dan was dedicated and efficient. Ed was 225 pounds of bubbling enthusiasm, a bundle of energy whose delight was to be surrounded by pre-teens. He was once characterized as "the only adult who could wear children out."

He died with his boots on, between talks at Our Lady of the Oaks, the last day of a retreat he was conducting.

Kathlyn will say, as many a Catholic has said about a priest friend, "Father is a member of the family." That is apt enough, I suppose, as a figure of speech, but can be only an approximation, for a Jesuit's true family is his Jesuit brothers-in-Christ. And yet my auxiliary "family" has meant so very, very much to me through the years, and they always will.

Thanks be to jazz, you do meet the nicest people.

Rev. I.L. Reason – An Unknown Great

*I*NCLUDED IN ANYONE'S TRANSITION PROCESS, when one has moved to live in another area, is the search for a good dentist. For me, an equally high priority is to find jazz musicians of my tradition, especially those who will allow guest players to sit in. When I found my dentist, I found both.

Dr. Lucius Doucet, who practices dentistry in Opelousas, about ten miles north of Grand Coteau, was recommended to me by a fellow Jesuit. He is not only an excellent dentist but a gracious gentleman and a dedicated recruiter for our retreats.

I first visited his office a couple of months after my arrival at Our Lady of the Oaks. It was through him that I came to meet the Reverend I.L. Reason – Lionel, to me and all his friends – a zealous minister and a super musician.

Dr. Doucet had finished tending to my dental needs and I was out of the chair, shaking his hand and saying thanks when it occurred to me to ask the question:

"Are there any good jazz musicians around here? I mean, who play traditional jazz?"

"Lionel," he said. "Lionel Reason. He's a preacher, and he plays great piano and sings. A black man. Real New Orleans style. You'd love him."

"Do you know if he allows other musicians to sit in and play a few numbers with him? I'm a jazz clarinetist – of sorts."

"I'm sure he would. Let's find out. Why don't you come to dinner with me and my wife? Bring your clarinet along, and we'll ask him. He plays at Toby's Little Lodge. It's a fine restaurant."

I met Lucius and his wife Harriet at Toby's Little Lodge, which is located a couple of miles south of Opelousas.

Genial Gene Paillet, the *maître d'*, whom I came to know and admire, greeted us. We entered the lounge area for a drink. There, at the piano bar, seated before a small upright piano and sporting a shining gold lamé vest and a blissful smile, was a consummate pro. I knew that after I heard a couple of his numbers. That night I knew I was in the presence of greatness.

Many a night thereafter I was privileged to sit in with him to enjoy and to learn. I learned much at the feet of this master. It amuses me to recall the many conversations we had between sets, when he wanted to talk theology and I (God forgive me!) was trying gently to steer the conversation onto music.

That first night I was welcomed with open arms.

"What do you want to play?" he asked.

"How about 'Moonglow'? Key of b-flat all right?" I responded.

"Do keys matter? Any key you want."

The astonishing musical odyssey of this genius would (and should) fill a book.

Irvin Lionel Reason was born in Plaquemine, La., in

1912. He began piano lessons at the age of seven under the tutelage of "Prof" Priestley, the music teacher and principal of Plaquemine Elementary School. By the time Lionel was eleven he was playing the piano at church and school functions. At age thirteen he was playing for pay in nearby lounges and honky-tonks.

A quantum leap in his playing ability occurred one summer when he was twelve. The school he attended was closed during the summer months, so he broke a window pane near the latch, opened the window, crawled in and had the first of many long practice sessions. When school re-opened, the broken window pane and signs of entry were detected.

"I had dusted the piano; I didn't have sense enough to leave it undusted. So they knew somebody had been playing it," he explained.

With the wisdom of Solomon, "Prof" Priestley made a decision:

"We'll wait and see who's improved the most, and we'll know who broke in and used the piano."

The circumstantial evidence proved to be overwhelming. Little Lionel was convicted. The sentence handed down was to play at school functions.

By the time he was eighteen, Lionel Reason broke into the big-time, joining the band of jazz giant Joe "King" Oliver, not long after young Louis Armstrong left Oliver to form his own band. Lionel was on the road with Oliver about five years. He left him in 1935 to form his own band in New Orleans, which stayed together about a year.

In 1936 Lionel joined Don Albert's big band in New Orleans and remained with him as pianist and arranger until 1939. Then he left Albert, again to form his own travelling band, composed mostly of New Orleans musicians.

World War II disrupted Lionel's personal life but not his musical career. In the Armed Services from 1943 to 1946, he was stationed in Aberdeen, Md., where he served with distinction as Entertainment Director.

During the post-war years Lionel returned to performing solo (pianist-vocalist), first in Detroit (until 1948) and then in New Orleans, on Bourbon Street. In New Orleans he also did some writing (arranging), the most notable example of which was Papa Celestine's classic recording of "Marie Laveau." He and his "adopted brother," the superb jazz drummer Freddie Kohlman, played on that recording. The New Orleans stay ended in about three years and was followed by a two-year stint in New Iberia, La., where he conducted his own music school.

The next fifteen or so years of his life were spent on the West Coast. First he joined "Wingy" Manone's Dixieland band. It was through "Wingy" that Lionel met Johnny Mercer, who, after becoming acquainted with Lionel's musicianship, announced one day: "'Kid' Ory needs you." Ory had somehow managed to lose his whole "book" (written arrangements). This presented no problem, of course, to Ory, but did for the musicians who, from time to time, replaced the departing musicians in Ory's combo. The solution was almost unbelievable: With Ory humming the parts and Lionel transcribing them, the "book" was restored!

Lionel remained with "Kid" Ory in San Francisco for about three years. It was during this period that his piano was heard with the Ory band in an early scene in *The Benny Goodman Story*, recording in that movie the transition from small combo jazz to the beginning of the big band swing era. Later, when Ory moved on, Lionel remained in San Francisco, doing a single at The Tin Angel.

Lionel's next move was to Portland, Ore., where he remained until 1969. It was during this stay that he felt called to the ministry. He became a licensed and ordained minister in 1968.

In 1969 he returned to south Louisiana, where our paths providentially crossed a few years later. He was then living in Baton Rouge and freelancing as a preacher in that area, commuting to Opelousas to perform at Toby's Little Lodge two nights a week, and driving to New Orleans in pursuit of a Master's degree at the Union Baptist Theological Seminary. It was my privilege to attend the baccalaureate services in New Orleans when he was awarded his Master's degree. A reporter from the New Orleans *Times-Picayune*, whom I had alerted to the possibility of a good human interest story, attended. He interviewed Lionel and paid him the tribute of a well-written story – only a fraction of this great man's due.

Since that day Lionel has spent less time at the piano and far more in the pulpit and in the classroom, as teacher (of Biblical studies) and student, pursuing the degree of Doctor of Divinity, which he attained in Houston in 1986.

His playing these days is confined mostly to private parties and social and civic events.

One of my fondest memories is of a night in December of 1973 in Lafayette, La. I was on stage in the Municipal Auditorium with the Ronnie Kole Trio. It was the first of three benefit concerts that Ronnie was kind enough to do for Our Lady of the Oaks. After I had played a couple of guest solos, I said to Ronnie and the audience:

"Before I leave the stage I want to acknowledge the presence of a dear friend of mine in the audience. A fellow minister of the Gospel and a great musician who has played with the likes of "King" Oliver, "Kid" Ory and Don Albert. A great pianist – Reverend Lionel Reason."

He stood up, and the spotlight found him. There was a resounding round of applause.

"Why don't you invite him up to play for us?" Ronnie asked.

I was surprised and delighted at the invitation.

"Lionel, come on up here," I said.

More applause followed as he walked jauntily to the

stage. He stole the show.

You made me what I am today / I hope you're satisfied... He sang and he played. It was one of his specialties, the jazz classic "The Curse of an Aching Heart." Thunderous applause. Then he and I did "Willow, Weep for Me." I felt a warm surge of joy that he had had this moment of well-deserved glory.

Ronnie shook his hand, thanked him, and praised him, especially for his vigorous left hand work.

"I wish I could do that," he said. "My left hand thinks it's a right hand."

And as Lionel left the stage, Ronnie said jokingly:

"Thank you. But don't come back!"

A roar of laughter rolled through the auditorium.

I often think wistfully of the Reverend Lionel Reason, who, with his wife, has taken up residence near Liberty, Miss. He is still quite active, but mostly in the ministry. I sorely miss him, as a man and as a musician – in that order.

Okay, Let's Face It...

*A*S I HAVE BEEN WRITING THESE PAGES, IT
has occurred to me often that I would, sooner or later,
have to address a question that must have arisen in the
minds of many of my readers. "So this Jesuit priest says
he is a jazz clarinetist. Just how good is he?"

It is a fair question and deserves an honest answer. I
will try to answer it, but I know it is next to impossible to
do so with complete objectivity.

One of my motives for wanting to address this question
is my fear that I may have conveyed the impression that I
think I deserve to be on the same bandstand with the great
musicians with whom I have played. On the basis of sheer
ability, I certainly do not. Yet I don't think I have ever
embarrassed them. I believe the truth about my presence
with them lies somewhere between my ability and their
benevolence.

In 1976 Angus Lind, a columnist for the New Orleans
Times-Picayune, wrote a column about my jazz exploits

and association with Pete Fountain and his Walking Club. In that article he posed the question to Pete Fountain. Pete's reply:

"He really loves to play. His sound, yeah, he has a good sound. But I think his feeling for jazz is his strong suit."

In another article about me Pete was quoted:

"Oh, he could make a living as a professional musician. On a scale of one to ten, I'd give him an eight."

I cherish that evaluation but suspect it is a bit too generous.

Another critique came from an outstanding New Orleans musician and successful businessman, Tony Valentino. I became acquainted with Tony in the 1960s, during my high school teaching days. Two of my senior English students were Tony's sons. Later, I came to know him better as a devoted Manresa retreatant and learned then that he had once been band director at Warren-Easton High School in New Orleans. One of his students was a slightly built teenage clarinet wizard named Pete Fountain.

I have the highest admiration for Tony Valentino as a man and as a musician and so welcomed the unasked evaluation of my playing that he offered me one night.

"You have a very good tone, and you play with great feeling, Father. That's it. That's you. Don't try to be anybody else. Don't try to be too fancy. That's not you."

I know these words are wise and true. I try to live (and play) by them. But I don't always do so. There are temptations to aim for high originality through improvisation (which is not my gift) or to crowd my solos with a profusion of notes. When I do this, I am failing to appreciate the wise words of the brilliant clarinetist Leon Roppolo:

"It's not *how many* notes you play, but *what* notes you play."

I am, of necessity, a limited musician. ("Musician" is such a formidable word; perhaps I should call myself a

Down through the years, I've had the pleasure of playing with a wide variety of talented musicians, mostly in southern Louisiana. **Above:** *The legendary Pete Fountain (left), Eddie Miller (center) and I play during a Christmas party in 1967.* **Below:** *My friend Joe Lamendola of Baton Rouge and I perform for the opening of Catfish Town in Baton Rouge in 1984.*

Two of the highly talented jazz musicians who always made me feel welcome to sit in and play with their groups are Ronnie Kole (left) and Pete Fountain (right). Here we are together for a dinner celebrating the 50th anniversary of my priesthood, in 2001.

Among the individuals and groups with whom I played down through the years are The Dukes of Dixieland (above) and the highly talented Al Hirt (left). The Dukes were formed in 1945 and have continuously replaced members who have died or left the band for other reasons. Among my most cherished friendships in the jazz music world was that of Frank Trapani (far right, holding trumpet), who died unexpectedly at a relatively young age in 1989.

Pete Fountain's Half-Fast Walking Club, which "marched" through the streets of New Orleans on Mardi Gras Day, starting in 1961, was made up of a truly motley crew, including yours truly. To provide some sense that we were an organized group, we dressed to fit different themes each year such as clowns, vikings and pirates, as shown in these pictures. The club was given its name by Pete's wife, Beverly, because she and some of the other wives of members thought our group was a sad excuse for a marching band. They felt we were completely devoid of precision or discipline – which was and is a fairly accurate assessment.

Musician and inventor Santy Runyon is one of the most intriguing people I met when I moved to southwest Louisiana to become a retreat director in Grand Coteau in the early 1970s. He was a designer and manufacturer of mouthpieces for clarinets and saxophones. His business, Runyon Products, is based in Opelousas and sells its merchandise all over the world.

Though I was less than happy with being reassigned from the bustling New Orleans area to the country village of Grand Coteau in 1971, I came to love my new home at Our Lady of the Oaks Retreat House. Here I am in 2002, in my third stint as a retreat director there, as I enjoy playing a tune on my clarinet in the peaceful courtyard of the retreat house.

Four of the Coco siblings gathered for a class reunion at Sacred Heart Academy in Helena, Arkansas, sometime in the 1990s. Left to right are: Mary Saia, Sarah Coco, Bro. Anthony Coco, SJ, and me.

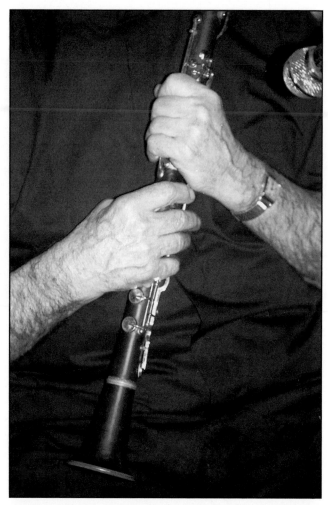

*My friend Rachal Bourgeois, originally from Opelousas, La.,
took this photograph of my 84-year-old hands holding my
clarinet while I was performing in New York City's Parker
Meridian Hotel in 2004. Rachal is the daughter of Dr. and
Mrs. George Bourgeois of Opelousas.*

"player" of music.) During my early years of Jesuit training, I was occupied and preoccupied with required studies. If I had been a professional musician, I would have been building an ample repertoire, keeping up to date with current tunes and developing my talent.

In my first two years of Jesuit life (the noviceship), except for the Christmas holidays and "long vacation" (two weeks), my clarinet case remained unopened. This was a time of strict religious and ascetic training, quite different from today's approach, incidentally. In the two-year period that followed we were immersed in the liberal arts – languages and literature (ancient and modern) – and were being trained in the spoken and written word. Music was appropriate enough to such a curriculum, but there was little time for it. On a private, minimal basis I kept in touch with the clarinet, but remained largely unaware of what was going on in the world of jazz and popular music.

The ensuing three years, when I had to concentrate on philosophical studies and English (my major), there was more time to play and some freedom to learn what was going on in the popular music world. The opportunities widened somewhat during the teaching period that followed (three years), when I taught English, Latin and French at Jesuit High in New Orleans.

It was during this time that I was able to organize a dance orchestra, recruited from the school band, which was under the direction of an accomplished musician, Prof. Michael Cupero. Prof. Cupero counted among his pupils jazz greats Louie Prima and Al Hirt. The talented youngsters I recruited were well-trained and eager to swing. Working with them was a satisfying outlet for me, but *they* did the public appearances while I remained proudly in the background.

Then my years of theological studies were spent in exile, or so it seemed to me, in eastern Kansas at St. Mary's

College, near Topeka. Two things kept my spirit afloat during those hard days: the prospect of being ordained to the priesthood, and a Jesuit trio. I was the clarinetist; my dear friend, Fr. John Snyder was the bass player; and the guitarist was Tony Brenner, who learned to play under Fr. Snyder's tutelage. We had many a happy session in our basement recreation room.

During the thirteen years leading up to my ordination, in 1951, I did acquire a fair repertoire, and to some extent did succeed in improving my tone, technique and improvisational skill. The same is true of the years that followed, when I was occupied, first, in high school teaching and then in retreat work. There were stretches of time, however, before I "went public" in 1966, when I went for months without touching my horn. Since that year I have been more consistent, but I accept the reality that, as long as I am in the active ministry, my music must remain only a glorified hobby.

Musically speaking, I am happy to be where I am today. I continue to add tunes from time to time to my repertoire, but often enough, when I am sitting in with the band, the leader will call a number or respond to a request, and I have to say I don't know it. The reaction is often one of surprise. Sometimes I manage to fake my way through it with reasonable success. At other times I wait and listen, or try to pick it up after a few choruses.

A word about my improvisational skill: I entered the world of improvisation in my early teens when I purchased by mail order for one dollar a book with the pretentious title *Improvising Simplified*, by one David Gornston. It was a landmark book in my musical life. The author introduced me to the mysteries of chords and chord changes.

What I learned from this book was the foundation on which I built what improvisational skill I have today, structured by what I have learned by listening to and imitating facile improvisers through the years. I think most, if not all, jazz musicians go through this stage before they reach a style of their own. Some never get beyond it. I am sure I am in that number.

Let me confess that my improvisations are hopelessly and happily traditionalist. Even bebop, frankly, is alien territory to me. And so much of contemporary jazz improvisation completely baffles me. These soloists seem to me to be instrumentalists expertly playing the final chapter in some advanced exercise book. An elderly jazz musician once said to me: "They playin' for themselves."

I listen with fascination and admire what I am hearing, but I do not quite enjoy what I hear, for the simple reason that I do not altogether understand it. I do not know how to play in that manner and am not sure I want to learn. I have settled for what I do. I stay always somewhere around the melody, embellishing it, weaving in variations of notes and phrasing.

I enjoy doing that. Many of my listeners apparently enjoy it, too. I must project that enjoyment, for time and again I am told: "You really seem to enjoy what you are doing." So we are all happy about it.

My philosophy of jazz playing, I must confess, doesn't go much deeper than that.

Santy Runyon: My Da Vinci

SANTY RUNYON, A LEGEND ALIVE AND flourishing at age 82, has been an important part of my musical life from the time we met in the early 1970s. He is my da Vinci, for he is not only an outstanding musician and a great teacher of the saxophone and all woodwinds, but an ingenious and versatile inventor and a resourceful manufacturer.

As I recall, we met in the lounge of Toby's Oak Grove Restaurant in Lafayette, La. In those days, Santy's band was playing in Toby's supper club five or six nights a week. Santy used to come into the adjoining lounge on his breaks, usually with his clarinet or one of his saxophones in hand, and play a few numbers with whoever happened to be performing in the lounge.

The night I met Santy, Al Terry (whose real surname, I was told, was Theriot) was holding forth in the lounge. Al was a big, burly man; he was disabled, and he performed from a wheelchair. His specialties were Country, Western and Cajun music, which he did admirably. He was also a versatile guitarist and vocalist, who had no trouble accommodating the likes of me as I sat in doing old standards, vintage ballads or jazz numbers. Santy walked into such a situation and jumped in with his unfailing enthusiasm on sax or clarinet.

"I used to take my breaks in the lounge and sit in. I was crazy," he once told me.

He may have identified the practice as craziness, but I see in it his zest for life, zest for playing, zest in all that he did or said.

This man of genius, who has lived in Lafayette, La., since the late 1960s, was born in Chanute, Kansas, in 1907. He grew up in a little oil town in Oklahoma. At age eight, he was the drummer in a small adult orchestra that supplied background music for silent movies in one of several theaters owned by his father. At ten, he blew his first notes on the saxophone. At eleven, he made a plastic reed for his saxophone, which – unless some claimant comes forward with proof to the contrary – must stand in history as a first. The young genius cut the reed from the hard-rubber front panel of a discarded Atwater Kent radio.

In his late teens, Santy went to college and majored in – what else? – music. He studied for two years at Oklahoma A&M (now Oklahoma State). The following two years he was at the University of Missouri, where he received his undergraduate degree. The following year he studied at the University of Tulsa, where he helped in the formation of that institution's first band.

All his life the man has been in the vanguard of *something*.

In 1931, fresh out of college, Santy went on the road with the famed Henry Busse band, his first venture into the big time. It was with the Busse band that he introduced the shuffle rhythm.

"I may have invented it," he once told me, quite casually.

He certainly pioneered it.

Phil Harris, whose band was riding high in those days, heard it in Galveston, Texas, as executed by the Busse band. Harris liked it and adopted it, thereby helping to spread it throughout the country. Later, Louie Prima's band thrived on it.

Santy left the road in 1933 and moved to Chicago, where he remained for nearly thirty years. Shortly after his arrival in Chicago he became the lead alto saxophonist in the Chicago Theater Orchestra and remained in that position for ten years.

It was during this period that one of his greatest gifts – that of teacher – came to the fore. He was and is an outstanding instructor in the flute and all the reed instruments. What began as a sideline blossomed into a full-time profession as he attracted more and more students, necessitating his resignation from the Chicago Theater Orchestra.

Runyon Studios opened in the "Loop" area. Later, branches appeared in Evansville and Villa Park. The contact that Santy made during those years with students, consultees and other musicians reads like a Who's Who of instrumentalists of the late 1930s, the 1940s and the 1950s. One of his star pupils was the great tenor man, Vido Musso. Bill Page, reed man with Barry Manilow, took lessons from Santy. Sonny Stitt, Paul Desmond, and a number of Duke Ellington's men – including Art Carney, Johnny Hodges and Jimmy Hamilton – came to Runyon Studios, some for instruction and others for consultation. Even the fabled "Bird," Charlie Parker, showed enough interest to drop in and learn from Santy.

The stories Santy has shared with me about his life in the world of music are legion – and fascinating.

There is the one about the saxophonist in the Kansas

City Nighthawks band who came to Runyon Studios for instruction. As a youngster, Santy lived for a while in Kansas City and looked up to and admired this band. And now here was a member of that band seeking help from him.

Another story has to do with Santy's invention of a way to mic a violin.

"I bracketed two orthophonic heads of record players to the violin, had a needle stuck in there, and it worked!" Santy said.

It happened at an outdoor concert in Fairyland Park in Kansas City in the 1920s.

"There was a big band behind the violin: five saxes, eight brass. But you could hear those jazz violin solos on the public address system all over the park," Santy told me.

In the early 1950s, when Stan Kenton's band was performing in Chicago, one of Stan's saxophonists made an emergency visit to Runyon Studios. He was just "not cutting it" with Stan Kenton. Stan had put him on four-weeks notice. Santy canceled some scheduled lessons and put him through a crash course that day. After the one-day program, the man showed great improvement.

"What happened to you?" Stan asked in amazement.

"I took a lesson from Santy Runyon."

"Well, go back to him. If you keep improving like that I won't have to send you back to the West Coast and get somebody else to come over here."

So, the guy kept his job.

An incident during the Chicago years eventually led to Santy's full-time career in the business of manufacturing mouthpieces for reed instruments. Santy's first production mouthpiece was for the baritone sax.

"When I played 'bari' in the Chicago Theater Orchestra, I couldn't hear myself. So I used to put chewing gum in the mouthpiece to build up the tone chamber. Some of the players said, 'Why don't you make a mouthpiece like that?'"

Santy accepted the challenge.

"The 'bari' mouthpieces in those days were big and bulky, because the first ones had been made out of wood. Then, you had them with a lot of bulky plastic material which I didn't need, because I decided to mold them. I bought some machinery and had a mold made. So I made the first streamlined mouthpiece. That was in 1941. The first sax player to use one was in the Tommy Dorsey band," Santy recalled.

It was a breakthrough. "Now, for the first time, you could really hear the 'bari' well in the sax section."

When Santy moved from Chicago to Beaumont, Texas, in 1962 his machinery went with him.

"I bought a ranch-style home with a two-car garage. One side of that garage was my factory. I produced mouthpieces on a small scale at first, then expanded to clarinet, alto, tenor – a full line."

Today, near Opelousas, La., stands Runyon Products. From this remote corner of the world thousands of clarinet and saxophone mouthpieces are shipped out to markets in the U.S. and abroad.

"I make mouthpieces for Selma and Conn. Bass clarinet mouthpieces for LeBlanc. I make sax straps for Yamaha. I make something – straps, mouthpiece caps, etc. – for just about all my competitors," he said.

One of Santy's proudest products, I suspect, is a single-reed bassoon mouthpiece, designed, patented and produced by Runyon Products – yet another Runyon original.

I once asked Santy how he came to move from Chicago to Beaumont, and from there to south Louisiana. His reply is a touching story that speaks volumes about Santy Runyon, not as a musician, but as a man, as a father.

"Well, I have five daughters. When the oldest daughter got to be thirteen I was running three studios in Chicago. How could I do that and keep track of five young daughters in such a big city? So I moved to Beaumont. I taught for a while at Lamar University. And I organized a four-piece jazz group. We played at the Petroleum Club there for seven years. Then, I moved to Lafayette, La., around 1969."

The Santy Runyon Quartet had come to Lafayette that year for a two-week engagement at Toby's Oak Grove, a supper club. Santy liked Lafayette so much that he never returned to live in Beaumont.

"I liked Lafayette and thought it was an even better place to raise five daughters," he explained.

Runyon Products, along with the five daughters, grew up in Lafayette. The business was later re-located to nearby Opelousas. Santy and his wife continued to live in Lafayette.

It was my good fortune that this great man's diverse and fascinating odyssey landed him in south Louisiana and so brought him into my life.

I cherish the fond memories of many conversations with Santy Runyon. His eyes shine and dance as he dredges up anecdote after anecdote from his fabulous past. The life of Santy Runyon is a fascinating subject in search of a biographer.

CHAPTER 24

A Sudden Sadness

*O*NE OF THE OUTSTANDING MUSICIANS I came to know, love and admire passed suddenly and shockingly from the world of New Orleans music and into eternity. His name was Dick Stabile.

He rose to fame as a bandleader and alto saxophonist during the 1930s, and later became the leader of the house band in the renowned Blue Room of the Fairmont Hotel (formerly the Roosevelt). Through the years his well-disciplined orchestra ably backed some of the nation's greatest performers: Tony Bennett, Ella Fitzgerald, Frankie Laine and Peggy Lee, to name a few. Dick once told me Ella was so pleased with the way his band had performed behind her during one of her runs at the Fairmont that she gave each member of the band a cashmere sweater.

"How much rehearsing do you have to do to back a musician like Ella Fitzgerald?" I once asked him.

"Not much," he answered. "We just went through her charts with her on a Sunday afternoon. Just a couple of hours. She loves my band."

A ring of pride was in his voice.

As one enters the lobby of the New Orleans Fairmont from the O'Keefe Street entrance, the imposing front door of the Blue Room, where Dick Stabile reigned for many years, is on one's immediate right. I came in that way one evening, a half hour or so before the beginning of the 9 p.m. show. I do not recall exactly where I was headed, somewhere in the nearby French Quarter. I had timed my arrival just to stop and say "hello" and have a brief chat with Dick Stabile. I knew the band would be on a break at that time.

Members of the band were in the lobby outside the Blue Room, standing in small groups, somber-faced and talking quietly. I sensed immediately that something was wrong. It was like a wake. It *was* a wake.

"Hi, Fr. Coco," one of the band members greeted me. "I guess you heard about Dick."

"No. What?"

"They found him dead in his room. This evening. We were waiting for him to show up. But he didn't. They found him dead in his room."

As I walked the length of the block-long lobby and out of the Baronne Street exit and across Canal Street into the French Quarter, I was in a daze. I wandered lost in the past, reviewing and cherishing memories of my always-pleasant encounters with Dick Stabile.

I can recall now when I first met him. It was in the off-lobby lounge adjacent to the Blue Room. The Ronnie Kole Trio was playing there, and I had come that evening to listen and to sit in. Dick came in on a break and Ronnie introduced him to me. In the course of his stay he complimented me on my playing.

"If you ever need a job, let me know," he said.

I laughed and warned him that I was not much of a reader. On a few occasions, however, he was kind enough to let me play a few solos in front of his band during dance sets. The band simply winged it behind me, a concession that touched me deeply, because this man was a musician's musician. He had a library of solid arrangements from which to draw, and he was a demanding drill sergeant of a bandleader, who, in no uncertain terms, settled for nothing less than precision – except when he was allowing me to do my thing.

I recall my dismay when I learned of the severe stroke he suffered and from which he never fully recovered. I remember the dogged determination that drove him back on the bandstand, fronting his band as always with his alto sax. Although he soloed occasionally, sadly, he was no longer playing quite like Dick Stabile. But the band was playing like Dick Stabile's band. He had a lifetime contract with the Fairmont. He honored it.

A poignant epilogue to my story of Dick Stabile happened some months after his death. The setting was Pete Fountain's Club on the third floor of the New Orleans Hilton. I had come in alone and had taken my favorite seat, at the end of the bar and next to the corner of the bandstand. I once sat there next to Liberace's brother, George. He was astonished when (more than once) Paul Famiglia, genial bartender and faithful employee of Pete Fountain for more than three decades, passed up to the band the usual drink-laden tray.

"Why, they're drinking on the job!" George said.

"The is New Orleans, George," I commented.

On this particular evening, as I sat at the bar before Pete opened his ten o'clock show, a lady left her table and came over. As she neared me I recognized her as Roseanne Stabile, Dick's widow. We exchanged greetings.

"I'm so glad you're here, Father. Are you going to play tonight?"

"I hope so. I don't know. Probably. Pete usually invites me up near the end of the show to do a couple of numbers.

Not always, though," I responded.

"I hope you do. I have someone here with me and I want him to hear you. He is a friend of Dick's from their boyhood days. They grew up together. He decided to come down to pay Dick a surprise visit. He has terminal cancer. Not long to live. He didn't know Dick had died. Please come on over and say hello to him," she said.

I walked with Roseanne to their table. There he sat, in a wheelchair, emaciated and smiling. I smiled back, shook his thin, feeble hand, and fumbled for words that I hoped would lift his spirits. After a brief conversation I promised prayers and gave him my blessing.

As I returned to my barstool I prayed:

"Lord, move Pete to invite me up to play tonight."

The Lord did. And Pete did.

I don't think I ever poured my heart and soul into "Summertime" and "Margie" as I did that night.

"So hush, little baby, don't you cry."

I played for Dick's friend. And for Roseanne. And for Dick.

CHAPTER 25

The Dukes of Dixieland

*F*RANK TRAPANI, WHO WAS ONE OF THE TOP jazz musicians on the New Orleans music scene, went from this life and out of mine as sadly and shockingly as did my friend Dick Stabile. Frank was, when I first met him, the lead trumpet player in Dick Stabile's band, a position he held for twelve years.

It was after he had left Stabile's band, during the dozen or so years that he played as "front man" for The Dukes of Dixieland, that I came to know him well and became very fond of him as a man and a musician.

Frank was a flexible musician, as capable and at ease reading the charts in a big band as he was freewheeling it with a small combo like The Dukes. He was a well-trained musician, having studied music at Loyola University of the South, the University of New Orleans and the Juilliard School of Music. He played with some nationally prominent bands before settling in with Dick Stabile's band in 1962. Frank joined The Dukes of Dixieland in 1976 and remained with them until his sudden death in June of 1989, at the age of fifty-two.

The original Dukes of Dixieland trace their origins back to the mid-forties, to two gifted teenage brothers, New Orleanians Fred and Frank Assunto. Fred was a trombonist; Frank, a trumpeter.

When I was a young Jesuit, not yet ordained, I attended a junior varsity football game one autumn afternoon. In the stands were two teenagers from the opponent's school, one on trumpet and the other on trombone, and they astounded me as they filled the air with rousing New Orleans jazz. I was convinced that I was listening to the nucleus of what was to be one of the best jazz combos ever to come out of the city.

For nearly twenty years Fred and Frank Assunto were the twin hearts of the outstanding jazz band, The Dukes of Dixieland. By the middle 1950s and on into the mid-1960s they were riding high on the national scene. "Papa Jac" Assunto, father of Fred and Frank, a versatile musician (banjo, tuba, trombone), had joined the band, as had vocalist Betty Owens, Fred's wife, billed as "The Duchess of Dixieland."

In 1966, at the height of their popularity, The Dukes of Dixieland were jolted by Fred Assunto's death from cancer at the age of thirty-six. They were staggered by his passing but recovered and re-grouped, and the beat went on.

The exciting beat of the original Dukes went on until, in 1974, the heart of Frank Assunto stopped beating. He was forty-two. The joyous music of the Assunto brothers – heard all over the world, in the U.S.A. and abroad, in live sessions (once in Carnegie Hall) and on numerous recordings – was laid to rest along with the body of Frank Assunto. I walked and played in that funeral procession up North Rampart Street.

However, the spirit of the music of the Assuntos – father

and sons – rose by the end of the year of Frank's death, when a new version of The Dukes of Dixieland was formed.

Entrepreneur John Shoup acquired legal title to the name, The Dukes of Dixieland. The resurrected Dukes had a home in the rooftop lounge of the Hotel Monteleone in the French Quarter, overlooking the Mississippi. The hotel's Skylight Lounge was re-christened "The Dukes' Place," and the beat was picked up again.

The first leader of the new band is a good buddy of mine, an accomplished trumpet and cornet player, Conrad Jones, formerly with Pete Fountain's band. With Connie and a cast of first-rate musicians, The Dukes were off and winging it again.

Through the years, leaders (usually trumpet players) and other members have come and gone. The performances of the different bands have varied from good to great. It has been my pleasure to have sat in with most, if not all, of them. I have always been made to feel most welcome in The Dukes' Place, and later, when John Shoup changed the venue to Mahogany Hall on Bourbon Street.

But back to my good friend, Frank Trapani. When he was the "front man" for The Dukes of Dixieland I sat in with them many times, both at The Dukes' Place and Mahogany Hall. The vision of Frank Trapani – giant-torsoed, bearded, playing with ease, power and beauty – will always live in my memory. And so will his kindness toward me.

When I heard of his death, I was stunned. A little bit of a blood clot on his lung carried the big man away. I mused, *How fragile we are, the strongest of us. We walk a fine tightrope over eternity.*

I wrote Frank's widow a letter of condolence, promising to celebrate a Mass for Frank, for her and their children. I was touched by her reply to my note:

"I know of you, even though we have not met. Each time you played with Frank, Frank would come home and say, 'Fr. Hot Chocolate played tonight.' He enjoyed that. He liked you a lot."

Sometime after I got that letter, I was in New Orleans and went to Mahogany Hall. It was during the Christmas holidays, two days before the Sugar Bowl game. A big and enthusiastic audience was there and the new Dukes were really sizzling. My good friends, for many years making up two-thirds of the Ronnie Kole Trio – bassist Everett Link and drummer Richard Taylor, recently inducted members of the band – were performing wonderfully well. Little red-headed Tim Laughlin, built like a jockey and playing like a giant – a guy with whom I walk and play in Pete Fountain's Walking Club every Mardi Gras Day – was on clarinet.

I felt very much at home playing with the band that evening. Tim and I lucked into an improvised duet on "Mood Indigo," which came off rather well and drew a good response from the listeners. It was a delightful evening, but edged with a sadness for me. I missed Frank.

CHAPTER 26

The Kings and I

DURING MY SIX-YEAR STINT AT MANRESA Retreat House, between 1976 and 1982, we had a retreat master exchange program going with two other Jesuit retreat houses, one in Missouri and the other in Minnesota. All three, coincidentally, share close proximity to the Mississippi River.

White House Retreat, as it is called, is perched beautifully on a high bluff above the Mississippi, downriver from downtown St. Louis. The retreat house in Minnesota is not on the river, but is on a lovely lake in a wooded area near St. Paul, in the township of Lake Elmo. Its designation is simply "Jesuit Retreat House," but the institution is popularly known as "Demontreville," because it is located on Demontreville Trail.

During that period of my life I made six or eight trips to the Twin Cities to give retreats at Demontreville, usually two in a row, which afforded me freedom between retreats, Monday to Thursday. My primary interest always was, of course, to try to find evening jazz spots, and if you look hard enough you can find traditional jazz anywhere.

Thanks to the entertainment section of the local newspaper and to Fr. Ed Sthokal, SJ (director of the retreat house) and to one of Ed's faithful retreat captains, I succeeded in finding jazz and enjoyed some pleasant evenings up there, listening to and playing jazz.

An ad in the St. Paul paper revealed that a spot in North St. Paul, Gulden's, offered a variety of live music, featuring Dixieland jazz one evening a week. The music was authentic and excellent. I was allowed to sit in, and I got along well with the musicians, musically and otherwise. Even the proprietor was inspired to unpack his accordion and jump in on some of the numbers.

We made one visit to the renowned Hall Brothers Emporium of Jazz in Mendota. The club was packed. I can recall seeing former major league baseball star Tony Oliva and his party there. The band was marvelous, transporting me in spirit downriver to New Orleans. It was the genuine article.

While I generally dislike direct self-promotion and usually manage to avoid it, I wanted to play with that band so badly that I waived my self-imposed rule and shamelessly asked to sit in. The leader agreed, but reluctantly. I played a number or two with them, and when I finished playing I was politely thanked and sensed that I would not be invited to play again that evening. I think that I played well enough to meet their standards, but since there are always musicians and would-be musicians in such places, eager to sit in, there is a fear, valid enough, of opening a musical can of worms that might alienate the patrons. That may have been their thinking.

In any event, I am glad I managed to worm my way in and can say I sat in with a band at the Hall Brothers Emporium of Jazz. All in all, it was not a bad experience.

By contrast, however, the receptions I was accorded by

the Wolverines Classic Jazz Orchestra and at Diamond Jim's Supper Club were cordial, even warm.

The Wolverines Classic Jazz Orchestra was a musical bonanza. We discovered them in a historic locale in St. Paul, the venerable old Commodore Hotel, a queen in her day, where F. Scott Fitzgerald was known to bend an elbow on many an occasion. The hotel had fallen on less prosperous times, but was functioning with dignity, catering to elderly permanent residents.

When we discovered the Wolverines the management had begun the project of restoring the Commodore Hotel to her former elegance. The Wolverines suited the old décor, for they played, and convincingly, the big band music of the teens and twenties, although they were all quite young. Their arrangements, which they reeled off with zest, were of that bygone era. It was a delight to listen to them.

I recall making several trips to the basement lounge of The Commodore with Fr. Sthokal and others. On our first visit I introduced myself to the young leader, whose hair was slicked back and parted down the middle in the manner of the twenties. I gave him my musical background and credentials, notably my association with Pete Fountain. This proved to be hint enough. I was invited to sit in. When I returned to The Commodore on several other occasions I was always warmly welcomed.

All the Wolverines were capable musicians, but not all were adept at playing without charts. Those who could accommodated me quite well, and we succeeded in making some good impromptu jazz. It was, to put it at its simplest, great fun.

I am grateful for those pleasant memories and was happy later to return the favor by putting their manager in touch with the promoters of the New Orleans Jazz and Heritage Festival, held annually at the New Orleans Fairgrounds every spring. A deal was struck one spring and they came down, played, and were well received. I was proud of them.

A touching bonus that came to me from my association with the Wolverines Classic Jazz Orchestra was the opportunity to meet one of the immortals of early jazz, trumpeter Jabbo Smith. Jabbo was attempting a comeback at that time. I saw and heard him featured with the band on two occasions that I can remember. On the first occasion he was not, of course, playing up to his reputed capability, but one could discern the greatness that was once his. The respect, even awe, that the young musicians showed him was moving.

The second public appearance of Jabbo Smith that I attended was a disaster. When he was introduced and mounted the bandstand that evening, it was immediately evident that he had had much too much to drink. He stood in front of the band at the edge of the bandstand, swaying unsteadily, confused. He managed to get through a solo, but was playing only on instinct and poorly. The young bandleader was distressed and uncertain about the way to handle the situation. Meanwhile, the band was doing a creditable job of covering up for him. I got up on the bandstand to lend a helping hand, bailing him out by playing along with him as best I could. After this ordeal our next move was to gently escort him to his seat. He resisted. He became belligerent. But finally he calmed down, to the relief of all present, as we got him to his table, a fallen giant.

After I had ceased making those trips to the Twin Cities, I often wondered what had become of Jabbo Smith. Then one day, I found my answer as I was paging through an issue of *The Mississippi Rag*, "the voice of traditional jazz and ragtime," a fascinating monthly published in Minneapolis. I came across a photo of Jabbo Smith and an obituary that gave him his due. I regret that I never heard him in his prime.

The most extraordinary experience I had during my visits to the Twin Cities happened at Diamond Jim's, a supper club in Lillydale. It was through the kindness of Pete Parranto, a resident of St. Paul, that this came about.

I met Pete on one of my early visits to the Twin Cities. He was the captain and recruiter of one of the retreats that I conducted at Demontreville. Pete, who was part owner of Diamond Jim's, invited Fr. Sthokal and me to accompany him and his wife Valerie to the supper club for dinner and music. It happened that the King Sisters and Alvino Rey were performing that week, staging two shows each evening.

I had long been a fan of the King Sisters and Alvino Rey (husband of Louise King). I recalled the annual TV Christmas specials featuring the King Family – a musical variety show with a crowd of King Sisters and their husbands and a host of children and grandchildren. It was a wholesome and delightful show.

As we approached the club from the parking lot, Pete was touting the food at Diamond Jim's.

"You eat some of our pike," he said, "and you'll forget about all that New Orleans seafood."

This struck me as pure rhetoric, of course, but I do admit that the food was quite good.

Pete secured an invitation for me to sit in with the house band, a small combo that played before the first and second shows. I had no problem hitting it off well with them.

We stayed for both shows and thoroughly enjoyed them. After the second show, when all the patrons had left, we lingered to meet the Kings and Alvino and share their company as they idled down and enjoyed their after-hours drinks and snacks.

At one point during my conversation with one of the King Sisters, she said to me:

"Father, I heard you playing with the house band. I really enjoyed it. Do you happen to know 'Mood Indigo'"?

"Oh, yeah. It's a great tune. I recorded it with the Ronnie Kole Trio," I responded.

"Play it for me," she said.

I reassembled my clarinet. As I began to play, softly in the low register at first, she began to sing. This caught the attention of her sisters. As we continued our *ad-lib* duet, they gathered around and began to sing in harmony. When we came to the end, Alvino announced that he wanted to join in the fun. He suggested that we move to the bandstand, where he could plug in his electric guitar. What followed was a jam session to remember. It was glorious! If only I had had a tape recorder with me that evening!

The last time I communicated with Pete Parranot was by mail during the years I was at Montserrat Retreat House in Lake Dallas, Texas (1988-1991). He wrote to remind me that it was a long time since I had been in the Twin Cities and had played at Diamond Jim's. He thought it was about time that I return. He inquired about the possibility of my taking off for a couple of weeks and returning for an engagement at Diamond Jim's. Maybe for a couple of weekends. There would be advance publicity. It was a kind and attractive offer, but we were never able to work it out. For one reason, I had too many commitments at that time over and above my regular duties in the retreat ministry. So I tabled the idea, but never really discarded it. Now it is one gig that will never come to pass. Pete died some months after my last correspondence with him.

Pete Parranto has left this world, but the memory of that glorious evening with him and Valerie and Fr. Sthokal at Diamond Jim's will always remain. And so will the memory of a good man whose kindness made it possible. May he rest in peace.

The finished manuscript

By Trent Angers, SFO

M Y ANNUAL RETREAT AT OUR LADY OF the Oaks Retreat House in Grand Coteau, La., had just ended when Fr. Frank Coco, SJ, approached me about reading a manuscript he had written. It was early November of 2005, the year before he went on to his great reward.

He knew I was a book editor and publisher, as well as an author. Only two years earlier I had interviewed him for a book I was writing titled *Grand Coteau: The Holy Land of South Louisiana*. He knew of my love for Grand Coteau and my respect for the Jesuits and all that they do.

Fr. Coco showed me a lime-green folder. It contained a modest-size manuscript of 114 typewritten pages.

"I've written this book. It's about my life as a jazz musician. A few of my friends have read it and said they think it ought to be published. I suspect they're just being kind, however," he said.

I reached out to take the folder.

"Let me see what you've got there, *Padre*," I said.

He handed it to me. I opened the folder and skimmed over the first page of the manuscript. It was written the old-fashioned way – on a typewriter, not a computer.

"Looks pretty interesting to me already," I said. "I'll be glad to give it a read."

Father Coco had a sparkle in his eye and a half-smile on his face as we talked.

"Well, I'd appreciate it, but I don't know if anyone would be interested in this except maybe my brothers and sisters," he said in his usual self-deprecating manner. "Look it over and get back to me, will you? No rush."

"Okay, sure. I'll be glad to," I said. "And, by the way, when did you write this?"

"Back in 1987 and 1988, while on sabbatical," he said, adding quickly, "but it's not quite finished."

"How much more time would you need?"

"Well, I'm not sure about that," he said.

"So, why not just take another sabbatical so you can wrap it up?"

"Sabbaticals are hard to come by these days, what with the shortage of priests..."

He went on to explain that he had tried to finish the book on a few occasions, but that the routine duties and responsibilities of a retreat director took up nearly all his time. He had managed to finish a few chapters since his sabbatical, but it seemed to him, and to me, that he would never achieve that sense of completion unless he took some more time off to think through and write those last few chapters – to the exclusion of virtually everything else.

We discussed, and agreed upon, the idea that one's best work is almost always a product of focus and concentration. No one can write a book by just pecking at it, writing an hour here, two hours there. It is necessary to create an environment with large, uninterrupted blocks of time in which the mind is free to roam, to explore the subject at hand, to write, rewrite, rethink, reflect, to enter into the world of the story, to the point that the story is all that is on your mind, and nothing else is vying for your attention.

In one of our conversations we agreed that the problem with trying to do two things at once is that you can't give your undivided attention to either. He knew that writing additional chapters would take all he had, and that doing justice to the job of retreat director and priest would likewise take all he had. If he were writing well, and really on stream, and the phone would ring and he'd have to stop what he was doing and attend to some duty that required his immediate attention, then he would lose his train of thought and the story would grow cold by the time he got back to it. Interruptions sever one's train of thought, but just being subject to interruptions prevents the writer from immersing himself in the deepest concentration that normally produces the best work. This is the conflict that Fr. Coco faced, and the reason why he feared the book might never be finished.

As I read Fr. Coco's manuscript I became more and more convinced of the value of his story. The uniqueness of his calling – as a priest, teacher, retreat director, musician and writer – had enabled him to connect with and minister to people whom few others could have reached. He had preached the Gospel through his musical talent, his kind demeanor and his nonjudgmental disposition, bringing the Good News to the most unlikely of places.

So, I called him and advised him that I found his manuscript to be quite meritorious, intriguing and well done.

Then I told him that, yes, we would publish it.

I also told him I was sure he could add another few chapters if he really wanted to, and if his schedule permitted. I added that I felt the book was essentially complete and that he should think of it as a success and let it go.

He had done what he set out to do, to tell the story of his jazz ministry, about how he loved the music and had performed with some of the best jazz musicians ever, counseled troubled members of the band, even heard confessions in an out-of-the-way booth at 2 in the morning, and made friends with many good people all along the way.

Moreover, I told him, you've written a valuable piece of the history of jazz and captured information that otherwise surely would have been lost. I cited his writings on Ronnie Kole, Pete Fountain, Al Hirt, the Dukes of Dixieland, Rev. I.L. Reason, Santy Runyon and others. Not to mention the unique adventures of a Jesuit priest/jazz musician who made his mark on Bourbon Street and elsewhere in south Louisiana – a story that is not likely to be duplicated.

"No need to write anymore, Father," I told him. "I think it's time to turn it over to the publisher."

Appendix 1

(Adapted from *Acadiana Profile* Magazine article, July/August 2008 edition.)

Why Everyone Loved Father Coco

A Jesuit priest and jazz musician, he touched the lives
of many who attended his retreats at Grand Coteau
and Manresa, as well as those who came to hear
his music in Bourbon Street nightclubs.

By William Kalec

The red cloth napkins are folded in the shape of a mitre – the
Pope's pointed head piece – inside the restaurant where the Italian dressing is named for Fr. Frank Coco, SJ.

It's a quarter past 10 a.m., so the crest of the lunch rush at
Poor Boy's Riverside Inn in Broussard isn't due for another
hour or so. The restaurant is quiet. The pace, a crawl.

A group of waitresses sit around a dining table, slouched in
their seats, small-talking about nothing in particular.

Kathlyn Hurst, the longtime proprietor of this place, sits
nearby with her back to the morning glare, speaking of something of great value to her – a friendship.

She and her friend met inside a smoky, martini-stained New
Orleans nightclub. This was decades ago.

Needing to get away from the frantic restaurant scene, Kathlyn had taken a weekend trip east to hear some jazz. The passage of time has clouded her recollection of the headlining act
– either Ronnie Kole or Pete Fountain, she guesses – but what
remains vivid in her memory is the Roman collar worn by the
clarinet player that night.

Kathlyn got the waiter's attention.

"Get the priest a drink," she told him. "Put it on my tab."

Father Coco ordered a scotch.

"He was not the type to just take a drink," Mrs. Hurst recalls
with a smile. "So he had to come over to the table and find out

my life story. I told him – and the rest is history. He was a part of our lives ever since. There was something about him that immediately put you at ease."

In a word, Fr. Coco was a priest who played a mean clarinet. He was a holy man who performed at unholy hours in unholy places on perhaps the most unholy street in the country, Bourbon Street. That's why newspapers and magazines wrote about him. That's why famous musicians called him up on stage.

Fr. Coco had a welcoming personality, a warm persona that drew people to him. He seemed to be supremely self-confident, yet truly humble at the same time. He was friendly, companionable and generous with his time and talent as a priest and jazz musician.

Fr. Coco was known to many as a retreat director at Our Lady of the Oaks Retreat House at Grand Coteau; he was stationed there three times for a total of 25 years, his last stint running from 1991 to 2006, the year of his passing. He was also stationed at Manresa Retreat House in Convent, La., for seven years in the 1970s and '80s. He taught at Jesuit High School in New Orleans for 16 years, from 1954 to 1970.

Those who were privileged to know Fr. Coco remember him with affection. In addition to fond memories of him, they each hold on to tangible things that remind them of him.

For Kathlyn Hurst, it's a mix of oil, vinegar and Italian seasonings. The salad dressing at Poor Boy's is a culinary legacy introduced by Fr. Coco and carries his name to this day. It takes her back to those Sunday nights when Fr. Coco dined at the restaurant, when they talked for hours over a hot plate.

For Dr. George Bourgeois of Opelousas, it's a photograph taken by his daughter, Rachal. It hangs in a black frame. The black-and-white portrait depicts Fr. Coco's aging, arthritic hands gripping the clarinet – a tool he used to preach the Gospel, not in words, but in chords.

For music legend Ronnie Kole, it's a song – "Just a Closer Walk with Thee," the signature tune Fr. Coco played in 1979 at Kole's father's funeral. The soft notes bounced off the cold mausoleums, Kole remembers. That fitting tribute was never forgotten, Kole says, his voice weakening under a sentimental rush.

For Dr. Steve and Joan Herbert of New Orleans, it's a manila folder of newspaper clippings and pictures documenting the life and times of their friend. Many of the clippings are yellowish around the edges, and the wardrobe in the photographs dates the era.

For Wilmot and Janette Ploger of New Orleans, it's the rings they wear on their left hands. Janette chose to convert to Catholicism prior to their marriage. Fr. Coco was the priest who guided Janette through the conversion process. In him, Janette confided her fears, her apprehension, how changing denominations would cause a rift in her Baptist family. Fr. Coco listened. He just listened. The Plogers have been married for 43 years. Fr. Coco baptized all of their children.

"If you asked, 'Of the people you know, who is most like God, or who would you want God to be?' I would want God to be like Father Coco," Mrs. Hurst says. "Because he was so warm and approachable. He always saw the better side of life. So, if God was a person, I'd want him to be like Fr. Coco."

* * * * *

The first time he heard it, Frank Coco loved the sweet sounds of jazz music. He was 8 years old at the time, a youngster growing up in Helena, Ark., a town on the banks of the Mississippi River.

Back then, African-American combo dance bands aboard riverboats cruising between Memphis and New Orleans would often dock in his hometown to perform.

The son of Sicilian immigrants and devout Catholics, young Frank began taking clarinet lessons from Sister Agnes Cecilia at age 11 – the genesis of the fusion of religion and music that characterized his celebrated life. He practiced insistently (five hours a day, he often claimed) on the horn his older brother, Sam, purchased for him for $3.50 from a pawnshop.

From ages 13 to 17, he played "professionally" in Helena, blowing for Lou Bell's Orchestra. His performances commanded $3 a night, $4 for bigger gigs. Even in the depth of the Great Depression, Frank realized drawing such a meager wage would make it nearly impossible to eek out a living through music. It would simply have to be his avocation.

The inspiration that directed him toward dedicating his life to the Lord came on any icy highway outside of Memphis in 1938. His brother Sam was driving the car and lost control. An accident ensued. Frank was ejected from the vehicle, onto the snowy pavement. By the grace of God, he was not seriously hurt. But the outcome of the accident shook him to the core.

At the time, he was playing music and working at the meat counter of a local grocery store. He lacked direction. He lacked ambition. Maybe, he thought, this was God's way of showing him a new path, a higher calling.

"I suddenly realized I was mortal," Fr. Coco once said to a reporter. "For the first time in my life, I thought seriously of the priesthood."

In June 1938, he sold his saxophone for $30 and used that money to purchase a ticket to Grand Coteau, La., where he joined the Society of Jesus. Two years later, he took his first vows. On June 14, 1951, his ordination to the priesthood occurred at St. Mary's College in St. Marys, Kan.

In 1954, Fr. Coco began teaching at Jesuit High School in New Orleans. He remained there until 1970. Students remember him as quite popular; he was known to join in during gym class activities and was quite the scholar in local prep sports. He never forgot a name, and he was always available if his students needed extra academic assistance.

During this stint at Jesuit, the reforms of Vatican II provided Fr. Coco the leeway to resume playing music for crowds – a secular pastime he surrendered upon entering the Jesuits. As Fr. Coco once stated:

"I'm grateful to Pope John XXIII who opened some windows to let fresh air into the Church, and I crawled through one of those windows, out into the jazz public."

Predictably, the sight of a priest in a New Orleans nightclub made for some interesting anecdotes. Like one time, a "spirited" patron slurred, "What would St. Ignatius think of a priest playing jazz in a bar?" Fr. Coco replied, "I think he'd dig it."

"He was 24 hours a day a priest," musician Ronnie Kole

says. "Music was a release but it was also a way for him to get a message through to people where they would listen to him and the collar didn't scare them away."

In fact, the collar was like an invitation to those seeking spiritual guidance. Fr. Coco occasionally heard impromptu confessions in bar booths and often suggested musicians attend his retreats at Grand Coteau or Manresa.

"I believe in being myself and not living up to someone else's image of what a priest ought to be," Fr. Coco told *The* (New Orleans) *States-Item* in 1976. "I don't buy that image a bit. I've had moments of prayer on a bandstand. There have been occasions when I've felt in a very prayerful mood while playing.

"I read a lot of loneliness on the faces of people who go into those places. They like to talk to you, and they begin talking to you as a priest."

There was also a lighter side to Fr. Coco's spiritual reach.

In 1965, he agreed to serve as chaplain in Pete Fountain's famous (if not infamous) "Half-Fast Walking Club" – a social organization whose principal contribution to society was dressing up on Mardi Gras Day, marching in the big parade, and consuming too many adult beverages. In fact, it was said, half-seriously, that Fr. Coco may have been the only club member who actually walked; the rest sort of stumbled and staggered.

Marching on Fat Tuesday was one of two instances in which Fr. Coco removed his clerical collar. The other was when he prepared his mother's recipe for spaghetti and meatballs. It was done from scratch. No shortcuts. The sauce, the meatballs, the pasta – they all had to be *just* right.

Sundays, of course, were reserved for the Lord. But Fr. Coco always found time to watch the New Orleans Saints. He was a huge fan.

On Sunday nights – in the years he was stationed in Grand Coteau – he'd regularly have supper at Poor Boy's Riverside Inn in Broussard, La., the restaurant owned by his friend, Kathlyn Hurst. He always brought his clarinet, and he seldom had to be prompted by the dinner guests to play a tune.

In 1987, Fr. Coco took a one-year sabbatical from retreat work to write his autobiography as a jazz musician, titled *Blessed Be Jazz*. Even with a 12-months leave, however, he didn't finish the book. He wrote a few additional chapters after the sabbatical and was hoping to write more, but his time ran out.

* * * * *

Lying in a hospital bed, Fr. Coco forced a smile when Rachal Bourgeois began joking about his famous spaghetti and meatballs. She smiled back. But Fr. Coco's eyes – now distant and saddened – revealed what that token smile could not mask: He wasn't ready to go. Even at 85, he wasn't ready for the sweet song of life on earth to end.

After battling heart disease, Fr. Coco died the morning of Sept. 7, 2006. The long list of those whose lives he touched came to pay their final respects at a service in New Orleans. Ronnie Kole was asked to play at the funeral. He accepted without hesitation, for it was Fr. Coco who eased his pain with a tune at Kole's father's funeral many years earlier.

The comforting sounds of "Amazing Grace" echoed throughout the church as a favor was repaid to an old friend. The teary-eyed attendees celebrated the life of a man dedicated to doing God's will, and the music played on.

Appendix 2

Key Dates in the Life of Rev. Francis J. Coco, SJ

Birth: Oct. 8, 1920, Helena, Ark.

High School: Sacred Heart Academy, Helena, Ark. (Class of 1937)

Entrance into the Jesuits: July 30, 1938 at St. Charles College, Grand Coteau, La.

First vows: July 31, 1940 at St. Charles College, Grand Coteau, La.

Ordination: June 14, 1951 at St. Mary's College, St Marys, Kan.

College: B.A. English, Spring Hill College, Mobile, Ala. (Class of 1945); S.T.L. in Theology, St. Mary's College, St. Marys, Kan., (Class of 1952)

Final Vows: Aug. 15, 1955, Immaculate Conception Church, New Orleans, La.

Family Information

Parents: Rosario Coco (Father); Giovannina Santo Colombo Coco (Mother)

Siblings: Sam, Vincent, Joseph, Sarah, Rose, Mary, Anthony and James

Principal Assignments

1945-1948, Regency, Jesuit High School, New Orleans, La.

1953-1954, Juniorate Instructor, St. Charles College, Grand Coteau, La.

1954-1970, Teacher, Jesuit High School, New Orleans, La.

1970-1971, Retreat Director, Manresa Retreat House, Convent, La.

1971-1976, Retreat Director, Our Lady of the Oaks, Grand Coteau, La.

1976-1982, Retreat Director, Manresa Retreat House, Convent, La.

1982-1987, Retreat Director, Our Lady of the Oaks, Grand Coteau, La.

1988-1991, Retreat Director, Montserrat Retreat House, Lake Dallas, Texas

1991-2006, Retreat Director, Our Lady of the Oaks, Grand Coteau, La.

Death: Sept. 7, 2006, New Orleans, La.

Appendix 3

Fr. Coco could cook!

Besides the ministry and music, Fr. Coco's other passion was cooking. His friends raved about his culinary skills, particularly when he cooked spaghetti and meatballs.

Musician Ronnie Kole recalls that while Fr. Coco kept a meticulous watch over the sauce, he always did so without his Roman collar, to keep it from getting stained. One of the few times he could be found without his collar was while cooking; the other was when he was dressed in costume and walking with the Half-Fast Walking Club during New Orleans Mardi Gras parades.

This recipe ran in *The* (Lafayette) *Daily Advertiser* on June 8, 1975.

See related photo on page 68.

Fr. Coco's Spaghetti & Meatballs

SAUCE
- 1 small onion, chopped
- 2 tablespoons of olive oil
- 2 6-ounce cans of tomato paste
- 1 heaping teaspoon of sugar
- Salt, to taste
- Pepper, to taste
- Basil, to taste

1. Sauté the onion in two tablespoons of olive oil.

2. Add tomato paste and seasonings; stir. Thin with water.

3. Cook down on low heat for about two hours.

MEATBALLS
- 1 pound of ground beef
- 1 cup of bread crumbs
- ½ cup of grated Romano cheese
- 3 eggs
- Parsley and garlic, finely chopped, to taste
- Salt, to taste
- Pepper, to taste

1. Mix all ingredients well and form meatballs.

2. Brown the meatballs lightly in a skillet to seal, then drop in sauce to complete the cooking. Cook for at least one hour.

3. Serve on cooked spaghetti.

4. Top with Romano or Parmesan cheese.

Note: Fr. Coco preferred to use Romano cheese, preferably freshly grated.

Index

Indexer's note: Page numbers in *italic* indicate photographs.

About the Author...

REV. FRANCIS J. COCO, SJ (1920-2006) was a Jesuit priest who spent most of his adult life in south Louisiana working as a retreat director, high school teacher and jazz musician. Using his clarinet, he performed extensively in New Orleans nightclubs and other venues, sitting in with some of the best-known jazz musicians of his time, including Ronnie Kole, Al Hirt and Pete Fountain.

Born into a large Catholic Sicilian family in Helena, Arkansas, in 1920, he entered the Jesuit novitiate at Grand Coteau, Louisiana, in 1938 and was ordained to the priesthood in 1951. He taught at Jesuit High School in New Orleans for 16 years. He served as a retreat director at Jesuit retreat houses for a total of 35 years, including 25 years at Our Lady of the Oaks in Grand Coteau, seven years at Manresa House of Retreats in Convent, La., and three years at Montserrat Retreat House in Lake Dallas, Texas.

His music is available on two CD albums: *A Closer Walk With Three* (With The Ronnie Kole Trio) and *Live From St. Louis: An Evening of Jesuit Jazz.*

Blessed Be Jazz is his first book.

Inspiring Books
from
Acadian House Publishing

Blessed Be Jazz
The Story of My Life as a Clarinet-Playing Jesuit Priest in The French Quarter of New Orleans

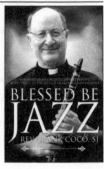

The 192-page hardcover autobiography of Rev. Frank Coco, SJ (1920-2006), a Jesuit priest who served for more than 50 years in south Louisiana as a retreat director, high school teacher and jazz musician. Using his clarinet, he performed extensively in New Orleans nightclubs, sitting in with some of the best-known jazz musicians of his time, including Ronnie Kole, Al Hirt and Pete Fountain. (Author: Rev. Frank Coco, SJ. ISBN: 0-925417-89-0. Price: $19.95)

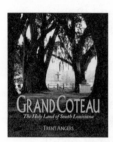

Grand Coteau
The Holy Land of South Louisiana

A 176-page hardcover book that captures the spirit of one of the truly holy places in North America. It is a town of mystery, with well-established ties to the supernatural, including the famous Miracle of Grand Coteau. Brought to life by dozens of exceptional color photographs, the book focuses on the town's major religious institutions: The Academy of the Sacred Heart, Our Lady of the Oaks Retreat House and St. Charles College/Jesuit Spirituality Center. The book explores not only the history of these three institutions but also the substance of their teachings. (Author: Trent Angers. ISBN: 0-925417-47-5. Price: $44.95)

Freedom From Fear
A Way Through The Ways of Jesus The Christ

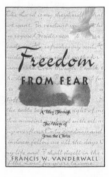

Everyone at one time or another feels fear, guilt, worry and shame. But when these emotions get out of control they can enslave a person, literally taking over his or her life. In this 142-page softcover book, the author suggests that the way out of this bondage is prayer, meditation and faith in God and His promise of salvation. The author points to the parables in the Gospels as Jesus' antidote to fears of various kinds, citing the parables of the prodigal son, the good Samaritan, and the widow and the judge. Exercises at the end of each chapter help make the book's lessons all the more real and useful. (Author: Francis Vanderwall. ISBN: 0-925417-34-3. Price: $14.95)

An Airboat on the Streets of New Orleans
A Cajun couple lends a hand after Hurricane Katrina floods the city

A 192-page book about a Cajun couple from Breaux Bridge, La., who took their airboat into New Orleans when the city flooded as a result of Hurricane Katrina. Doug Bienvenu, the airboat operator, and Drue LeBlanc, who was suffering with kidney disease, rescued hundreds of people during their 3-day mission of mercy. (Author: Trent Angers. Hardcover ISBN: 0-925417-87-4. Price: $16.95. Softcover ISBN: 0-925417-88-2. Price: $14.95.)

TO ORDER, list the books you wish to purchase along with the corresponding cost of each. Add $3 per book for shipping & handling. Louisiana residents add 8% tax to the cost of the books. Mail your order and check or credit card authorization (VISA/MC/AmEx) to: Acadian House Publishing, Dept. B-55, P.O. Box 52247, Lafayette, LA 70505. Or call (800) 850-8851. To order online, go to www.acadianhouse.com.